G

Tom Miko

Author: Tom Miko

First edition

Copyright, All rights reserved!

The book may not be reproduced or published in any form or sense, electronic or mechanical, including public lecture or course, audiobook, any internet communication, photocopying, recording or any form of information recording, in any form or sense, without the author's written approval.

Copyright: © Tom Miko, 2024

Table of contents

Introduction

Lock, Stock and Two Smoking Barrels (1998)

Snatch (2000)

Swept away (2002)

Revolver (2005)

RocknRolla (2008)

Sherlock Holmes (2009)

Sherlock Holmes: A Game of Shadows (2011)

The Man from U.N.C.L.E (2015)

King Arthur: Legend of the Sword (2017)

Aladdin (2019)

The Gentlemen (2019)

Wrath of Man (2021)

Operation Fortune: Ruse de Guerre (2023)

Guy Ritchie's The Covenant (2023)

References

Introduction

Guy Ritchie's name needs no introduction to most movie lovers. He is one of the world's best-known film professionals, who has directed many great productions during his more than 25-year career, and has brought more than a dozen outstanding works to the table. Today's 30 and 40 years olds, who were teenagers or in their twenties when he burst into the public consciousness with his first films around the turn of the millennium, can still remember the impact of his works.

My friends and I often quoted from his movies, more than once our conversations were colored by the mention of one of the dialogues he created, we knew many scenes by heart and often recalled them. They were defining films of our young years, with which we not only had a good time, but also had a moral lesson for us, we learned that those who enter the path of sin should not expect much good. It was also a great help to our parents, because we owe a good part of our upbringing to similar films - with lot of educational parts - including the works of the director, in which both the good and the bad always receive their final reward.

If the movie *„Actually Love"* were made today, Hugh Grant as the Prime Minister of Great Britain would probably say the following in that particular scene at 10 Downing Street:

„We may be a small country, but we are a great one. A country of Shakespeare, Churchill, The Beatles, Sean Connery, Harry Potter, David Beckham's right foot, David Beckham's left foot come to that..., and of course we have Guy Ritchie."

And to this day, my brother and I often mention one of *„Snatch's"* funniest scene when talking about England's capital, which goes like this:

„Yes, London. You know: fish, chips, cup 'o tea, bad food, worse weather, Mary f@cking Poppins... LONDON."

(Of course we both love and appreciate this amazing city and British people too…)

Guy Ritchie was born on December 10, 1968 in Hatfield, Hertfordshire, England, and knew at a very young age that he wanted to be a film director. He never went to a film school, developed himself individually and got to where he is now on his own. In the beginning, he made advertising videos and promotional materials for musical bands, then he put his earnings aside and created his short film „*The Hard Case*", which is the prequel of his first real film. Trudy Styler, the wife of the popular British singer Sting, saw the film and then thought that she would invest in Ritchie's first feature film. The rest is history from here.

Although it was not easy for him at the beginning of her career - especially as a young director who was initially rejected by most studios - his uniqueness, incredible work ethic, humility and love for films brought him success. Since then he has been producing better and better movies for the audience year by year. Let this book be a kind of tribute to Mr. Ritchie, who dedicated his life to the film industry and to entertain, make people think and teach millions with his creativity and unique, incomparable style and thereby make the world a little better place.

I wish you a good reading!

„My principal job is to make interesting and entertaining films, and I'm not proud of which format or which particular technique I use. I just wanted the film to look good." – Guy Ritchie

Lock, Stock and Two Smoking Barrels (1998)

Guy Ritchie's first direction can definitely be considered a cult film. The Lock, Stock and Two Smoking Barrels is a British action comedy based on criminal elements released in 1998, which immediately launched the career of the now world-famous English film director. In some professional circles, it is placed on the same level, both in terms of its category and impact on the film world, such as Tarantino's *"Pulp Fiction"* or Danny Boyle's *"Trainspotting"*. With this film, not only the director, but also the British proved that they can produce a really good low-budget blockbuster. All it takes is a great story, an excellently written script, talented actors, as well as dialogues based on London dialect and a big dose of English black humour. And of course a brilliant director who mixes it all up. The rest of it would take care of itself and one of the most entertaining British movie of all time was born.

The story was also written by Guy Ritchie, but he has not yet taken on the role of producer here, it was mainly done by Matthew Vaughn, who also appears in the film and who was responsible for the production of many films since then *("Snatch", "Kingsman"* films, *" Rocketman")*. In addition to the director, this film also brought international fame for two good childhood friends. They are none others than Jason Statham (the star of the films *"The Transporter"*, *"Expendables"* and *"Fast and Furious"*), **(illustration 1a)** the dedicated fan of oriental martial arts and diving, and the former English national team footballer, Vinnie Jones *("Gone in 60 Seconds", "Mean Machine")* **(illustration 1b)**.

Along with them, young actors of the time appeared who mostly played in British series before and now have more than 100 productions behind them. Such as Jason Flemyng *("Stardust", "The Curious Case of Benjamin Button")*, Nick Moran *("The Musketeer", " Harry Potter and the Deathly Hallows Part I-II")* or Dexter Fletcher, who is also a director now *("Band of Brothers", "Eddie the Eagle", "Rocketman")*.

Together with Statham, they are the 4 good friends **(illustration 1c)**, who, due to a card party gone wrong, find themselves in the deepest recesses of the London underworld, who have one week to give 500,000 pounds to the well-known mobster, Hatchet Harry *(" P.H. Moriarty" - "Jaws 3-D")*, he is the person you do not like to owe **(illustration 1d)**. This is where the real plot of the film begins, this is where this British epic -which can hardly be called slow -, becomes interesting, this is where the many complications and the flow of events starts. Cinematography was done by Tim Maurice-Jones, who also makes a brief appearance in the film. He is the one whose head was pressed into a barrel of water by Harry's right hand man, Barry the Baptist, who played by former boxer, bouncer and bodyguard Lenny McLean, who died of cancer shortly before the film's premiere **(illustration 1e)**.

In terms of the location of the Lack, Stock and Two Smoking Barrels, it takes place in London, mostly in buildings and rarely in front of them or on the street. Many shots were recorded in seedy apartments, where more people than necessary do business, shop or live together. Whether the stay is temporary or just for a quick hustle in these relatively small spaces is not always clear in some cases **(illustration 1f)**. Places that evoke such a typical 90s atmosphere are, for example, the boys' crib or the hideout of the rival gang. But many scenes take place, for example, in JD's pub, whose owner is namely the father of the boy who lost the card game, played by none other than the singer-songwriter pop icon, Sting **(illustration 1g)**.

According to Ritchie and casting director Celestia Fox *("Der Name der rose," "Little Shop of Horrors")*, casting took quite a long time as they tried to find the best person for each role. For example, Sting's decision to take on the role of JD was determined by the fact that he really liked the director's previous and also first film work, which was the previously mentioned short film *"The Hard Case"*.

The casting therefore went excellent, the end result was worth the time spent. Perhaps it was so much easier for those involved, that most of the characters are also not at the top morally, so there was no need to look for very different actors who fit extreme personality types and could shape them. Most of the characters give the impression of a thug, a bad boy, or someone who is always in something illegal and who does not shy away from swindling, and this does not apply to the actors, but of course to the characters. In the film, almost everyone drinks, smokes, swears, and tries not to earn a living in the most legal way **(illustration 1h)**.

The characters represent different levels of crime, one way or another, but nobody innocent at all. Apart from that, the main characters, the four calfish, mid-to-late twenties, up and coming guys from London, are really lovable characters for who you can get excited about during the 1 hour and 47 minutes of playing time. A few years before the film, in a drug-soaked film starring Evan McGregor, I already had a similar feeling, but unlike many, I don't want to get into more comparisons now, I think Guy Ritchie suffered enough from this when the movie came out. So yeah, come to think of it, I can't get around that if I want to get my train of thought across, so I'm not even going to try. So both there and here the emphasis is somewhat on friendship, common suffering and dealing with life's trials together, preferably supporting each other, but still in a different way. And somewhere the director managed to bridge this and solve it in such a way that it cannot be the same template or pattern to pull on the two teams. Yes, they are similar, but still different. In „ *TP* " the drugs, here gambling is to blame, **(illustration 1i)** but yes, what they have in common is human frailty, weakness and the desire for sudden pleasures, satisfaction or enrichment.

So, most of the criticisms against the director are mostly exhausted in this comparison, as well as in the fact that, in addition to the *"Pulp Fiction"* and *"Trainspotting"*, he also drew something from other, mostly earlier British crime films. But if he did - which I doubt anyway, because the originality and inventiveness of the film does not support this - who has the right to hold him responsible if the end result was simply so brilliant? And yes, after Quentin and

Boyle's masterpiece - which was followed by many clones the following year - this work is not a little brother among many, but capable to show something new and original, even if - in terms of its genre - there is no doubt that is closer for the aforementioned director mages cult movies than anything else.

What might still be in common - and I stopped this line of thought here -, is that all three films started or restarted many careers, even though none of them was a huge box office success by today's standards, but there is no doubt that each of them produced good numbers. When it was released in English cinemas, people under the age of 18 were not allowed to see the film. The director was rather confused about the matter and said:

"There is not a single nude scene in the film and the word c@nt is only used twice. It's true that the f@ck is at least 150 times, but I thought we could easily go up to 200."[1]

Edited by Niven Howie *("The Hitchhiker's Guide to the Galaxy", "Resident Evil" films)*, and $1.35 million budget movie paid off handsomely for Summit Entertainment, The Steve Tisch Company, and SKA Films, grossing around $28 million produced worldwide so far.

---

[1] pl: Lock, Stock and Two Smoking Barrels, Cinema magazine. Budapest, 1999/5, 67. pages.

The unique music found in the film was provided by two Liverpool-born composers, named David H. Hughes *("The Bachelor", "Bob the Butler")* and John Murphy *("28 Days Later", "Guardians of the Galaxy Vol. 3")*. Thanks to them, the music selection has become truly unique, since almost every genre, from the soul hits of the 60s and 70s to reggae music and the London underground of the time, is represented. The continuously pulsating chords form a perfect blend with the visual world, creating a video clip-like effect in some scenes **(illustration 1j)**. The carefully selected tracks perfectly support the events, thus making the movie even more exciting and diverse, but also unique. The film debuted on 23 August 1998 at the Edinburgh International Film Festival and was nominated for the British Academy Film Award in the outstanding British Film of the Year category that same year. In 2000, Ritchie won an Edgar Award from the Mystery Writers of America for Best Motion Picture Screenplay, and in 2016, Empire magazine ranked this great piece of work 75th in its list of the 100 best British films and the editors had a great opinion of it.

In my personal opinion, this is roughly what a good action-packed gangster movie should be, which isn't so bloody serious that it can't contain several humorous scenes. These are perfectly balanced in the film, in addition to the drama and action, there are plenty of jokes, most of which come from the exceptionally good dialogues. You can't get bored with it for a minute, and this is can largely thanks for the excellently written story and flawless direction, the varied music and, of course, the colorful characters. I saw the film for the first time when I was still in high school, at the usual Thursday night dormitory movie night, shortly after it was released on VHS and it has been one of my favorite ever since. I watch it again every few years and the old memories always come back, I really like that feeling. Therefore, those who like fast-paced, action-packed, plot twists, humorous films with excellent music and haven't seen them yet will definitely have fun watching Guy Ritchie's first feature-length film.

1a

1b

1c

1d

1e

1f

1g

1h

1i

1j

Snatch (2000)

The second feature film of the English director genius, the British American crime thriller and black comedy Snatch, which was released in Great Britain on August 23, 2000.

The great success of *"Lock"* set the bar high, but Ritchie seems to have managed to jump it. At the time, many thought it was a sequel to his first film, as it shows some similarities with in its structure, visual style and atmosphere, but this one has a darker tone and is much more satirical and, one might say, it is also more violent. But at the same time the funny elements, the funny characters and humorous dialogues somewhat compensate for this, so it is not a gray thriller or crime, but an extremely entertaining work.

The similarity between the two films is further enhanced by the fact that many actors who have already shown their talent in the previous cinema were given roles in this one as well. For example, one of the film's main characters, Jason Statham, who plays a spiv illegal boxing bookie nicknamed "Turkish", **(illustration 2a)** and his childhood friend Vinnie Jones, who this time also plays a tough guy, "Bullet-Tooth" Tony, as well as Alan Ford, who, although he was only a narrator in "Lock", is now one of the central figures in the film. He took on the character of Brick Top, the dreaded and ruthless gang boss of the London underworld. In addition to them, of course, there are many great actors in the film, for example, Brad Pitt (he needs no introduction, I think), who plays the gypsy wrestler "One Punch" Mickey **(illustration 2b)**, incredibly well, the role was simply made for him, no one else could have played it so well, I'm sure. There's also Benicio Del Toro *(the "Sicario"* films*, "The Usual Suspects")*, who perfectly portrays Franky Four Fingers **(illustration 2c)**, as well as Jason Flemyng (Darren), who is Mickey's right-hand man and who also starred in Ritchie's debut film.

Plus, we also have to mention Stephen Graham, who plays Tommy, the somewhat incompetent friend of Turkish. Before that, Graham mostly appeared in short and TV films and series, and whose career was also launched by Ritchie, since then the public has seen him in many large-scale productions (*"Pirates of the Caribbean"* films) **(illustration 2d)**.

The screenplay was also written by Guy Ritchie, which was so well done that it is already a reason for someone to watch the film and it is not a coincidence that the story got its own series more than 15 years later. The production debuted in 2017 with Rupert Grint *("Harry Potter" movies)* in the lead role and as an executive producer, and has two seasons until now. The main producer of the 1 hour 44 minute film with a production budget of approximately 6 million pounds was Matthew Vaughn this time as well, but he no longer took on a role here.

The story of Snatch runs along two main lines, the central element of which is an almost priceless 86-carat diamond the size of a walnut, which the many dubious figures and underworld characters of course want to get **(illustration 2e)**. There are illegal boxing matches, dog fighting, robbery and many forms of violence. Watching the film, you can almost smell the sweat of enforcers suffering from testosterone overflowing, petty criminals or profit driven gangsters dazed from drug or alcohol coming through the screen. The narration of Turkish provides a great framework for the story, just like in Lock, this method has worked for the director here as well and it works great. Time in this movie is not necessarily linear in all cases, and it is possible that at first watch the many events seem a bit confusing and it is also conceivable that the whole picture comes together in one's head only after many viewings. However, if you have it, it can equal an aha experience. The fact that the plot takes place again in the background, with the introduction of many seemingly separate events and numerous characters, then with their meeting later, be fulfilled somewhere in the not too distant future, also speaks to the director's genius. Not to mention the compilation of one of the funniest casts. It would be difficult to talk about the main starting point of the story without spoilers and do the more detailed presentation of the plot, so I would skip this for now and focus a little more on the characters. I can tell that much that similar to *"Lock"*, here there are up-and-coming criminal seedlings - , who happen to be Turkish and Tommy - after a deal gone wrong, suddenly cause some trouble for one of the most feared figures of the London underworld **(illustration 2f)**.

Which of course thanks to some threat, they treat it with sufficient seriousness and try to fix the sudden problem as quickly as possible and get off with a whole skin of this situation. During their efforts towards this and in the chain of events and the development of the plot itself, their decisions, their ability to recognize the situation and their survival instinct are key. They try to do everything to have the best possible outcome of the matter, that is, to get out of the tight state, in which they ended up somewhere through no fault of their own. In addition to Jason Statham, I think that Brad Pitt is the other main character of the film, but maybe I just think that way because of their brilliant acting and actually the film doesn't even have a central character. If we think about it more, none of them are highlighted at the same level as is usual with a main character to do. By the way, Pitt could easily have applied for the best actor Oscar in 2001 for his portrayal of Mickey, at least in my opinion. Because of his Irish nomadic gypsy accent, the creators created special English subtitles for his scenes, which was quite rare until then. There is no doubt that the two of them carry the film on their shoulders, excellently portraying the characters written for them, but no one can say a single bad word about the other actors either, they all did a good job **(illustration 2g)**.

In the middle of the complications, in addition to the central characters, we also get to know a number of side characters, most of whom have an impact on the progress of the story in one way or another. Be it the three doltish African-American robbers, Vinny (Robbie Gee - *"Mean Machine"*, *"Underworld"*), Tyrone (Ade - *"The 51st State"*, *"Casino Royale"*) and Sol (Lennie James - *"Jericho"*, *"The Walking Dead"*) **(illustration 2h)**, Boris The Blade, the Russian (Rade Serbedzija – *"Eyes Wide Shut"*, *"Space Cowboys"*) or Cousin Avi (Dennis Farina – *"Get Shorty"*) **(illustration 2i)**, everyone shapes the story at their own level and with their own set of tools. Each character has something unique and at the same time strange, which makes the film even more interesting, and almost all of them have a nickname, which helps a lot in identifying them in the new scenes. In the film, the dog (by Mickey: dag) named Daisy, also plays an important role, we can thank him for several funny scenes **(illustration 2j)**.

Ritchie thus proved that the success of his previous film was not a coincidence, and the critics were forced to acknowledge this, both then and now. True, there were also negative opinions that the film starts slowly, as if it doesn't find itself in the first 15-20 minutes and that the story is sometimes confusing. On the other hand, I think (and this is not just my opinion) that if you pay attention to what is happening, you will not only be able to put the puzzle together, but you will also be able to enjoy this great work, among other things, because after put the individual parts together and understood, it can also be a great feeling of success. By the way, no one has to strain themselves to do this, if you watch the film calmly and feel the atmosphere, you will really understand why what is happening and even have fun in the process. Overall, the film received good reviews, and its income figures are not to be neglected, as it has earned roughly 83 million dollars worldwide so far.

The music inserts, which this time were also great and perfectly suited to the freer use of the camera, and which tracks, like the *"Lock"*, from techno to slower tracks, are also selected by John Murphy. The relatively fast pace was taken care of by cinematographer Tim-Maurice Jones, who previously worked with Ritchie, with the help of editor Jon Harris *("Stardust", "Kick/Ass")*. Ritchie got the hang of playing with the camera, this unusual style worked great in this film too. „Camera movement can also make objects seem sharper and more vivid than in stationary framings. Certain camera movements give bodies greater solidity. This is apparently one reason modern directors like to circle around the action, as in the opening scene of Reservoir Dogs."[2]

The film was produced by Columbia Pictures and SKA films, and is mainly distributed by Columbia TriStar and Sony Pictures. I would definitely recommend it to anyone who hasn't seen the work yet, because it's really rare to have such a cinematic experience. The story, the atmosphere, the humor and the characters, as well as the excellent acting work, make this one of my top 10 favorite movies, just like the *"Lock"*. What I also think is important is that before Snatch you should also watch the *"Lock"*,

---

[2] David Bordwell, Kristin Thompson, Jeff Smith: Film Art – An introduction. Twelfth edition. McGraw-Hill Education, 2020. 199. pages

not because it is a continuation of the story, but definitely from the point of view of the visual similarity and of course for the great experience.

2a

2b

2c

2d

2e

2f

2g

2h

2i

2j

Swept Away (2002)

After the overwhelming success of *"Lock"* and *"Snatch"*, Guy Ritchie rowed into new waters (literally) and directed his third film, Swept Away, a romantic comedy set partly on water and partly on an uninhabited island, which released in autumn 2002. With the exception of a small group of fans (such as myself), most viewers and critics felt that this work should not have been born or not this way.

The movie is a remake of a 1974 Italian film of the same name, starring Giancarlo Giannini, the father of the film's protagonist, Adriano Giannini, who plays Pepe. While people liked the original film overall, Swept Away, which debuted in Los Angeles on October 8, 2002, failed to live up to expectations. In addition to that it was a huge flop at the box office - it brought back roughly a tenth of its $10 million production budget - it caused a general public outcry also, among women in general. The other main character of the film is Madonna, who embodies the spoiled lady Amber, who was the director's wife at the time **(illustration 3a)**. Alongside them Bruce Greenwood, Elizabeth Banks and Jeanne Triplehorn, as well as David Thornton also appear in the movie **(illustration 3b)**.

The original story was written by Lina Wertmüller, who also directed the 1974 film, and along with Ritchie, she also contributed to the story of the remake, so the two of them wrote the script for this nearly one and a half hour movie. The producer this time was also Matthew Vaughn, furthermore David Reid and Adam Bohling, who later worked together as co-producers in many productions (,,Layer Cake", ,,Kick/Ass"). They took on the responsibilities of making the film under the auspices of the Screen Gems, the SKA film and the Codi S.p.a studios.

In terms of the story of the film, it is therefore completely identical to the original work, according to which three classy couples, who take part in a private yacht trip in the Mediterranean, are heading from Greece to Italy **(illustration 3c)**. The guests, who are used to prosperity, have a carefree time and enjoy the service, but nothing is good enough for Amber (Madonna), who is extremely spoiled and very conceited. She keeps dissatisfied, and constantly makes insulting remarks about the young, handsome fisherman Pepé, who works on the ship **(illustration 3d)**. Sometimes she complains about the food, sometimes about the boy's cleanliness. He humiliates her on several occasions in front of the guests and the ship's crew and jiggle him all the time. About halfway through the film, the turning point comes when

Amber asks (almost orders) Pepé to take her by boat after her friends, who left her on board the ship for a short time during the day because they went on a little getaway nearby **(illustration 3e)**.

The man and the women who don't particularly like each other, who are completely different in personality, manners and, of course, social status, get into a storm, and after a while find themselves on an uninhabited island, far from civilization. The other half of the film takes place in this beautiful environment, where you can hardly see anything but the sky-blue sea and sandy beach. The two protagonists suddenly find themselves depending from each other, especially Amber, who until then lived a carefree rich life, while Pepé was always busy and did manual work **(illustration 3f)**. So the roles changes, if the woman wants to survive, she has to listen to the boy and if she wants to have a good relationship with him, she has to change her manners too, which of course she doesn't like at all **(illustration 3g)**.

As already mentioned in the introduction, critics had an extremely negative opinion of the film. According to Roger Egbert, the late excellent film critic, although the film is a relatively faithful remake of the original, still has many flaws. According to him, most of the characters traveling on the ship are haven't written good and are not felt by the actors, according to other critics, they are more like caricatures that are not presented sufficiently.

According to the film critic, the problem with Amber's character is simply that she starts off in such a repulsive way right at the beginning of the film - and then carries it on until roughly the middle of the film - that she is unable to turn it around by the second half and the end of the film, Madonna unable to shape her into even a minimally likable individual. Of course, it is impossible to know how much of this is the pop singer's superstar and how much is her late husband's fault. Of course, the negative opinions did not stop at Madonna's acting skill.

According to the naysayers, Elizabeth Banks *("The Hunger Games", "Cocaine Bear")*, - who has already proven several times that she is a talented actress and lately director also - , is the only one who is faithful to her role. In this case she plays a silly but hot young girl **(illustration 3h)**, her playing is relatively acceptable, while

Jeanne Triplehorn- for example *("Basic instinct", "The Firm")*, got a hard work **(illustration 3i)**. According to some critical opinions, he is not really a supporting character, more like a prop, and Bruce Greenwood *("Star*

Trek" films) does not shine too much in the role assigned to him, rather he just get over his lines, but nothing more **(illustration 3j)**. It's true that they didn't get too much time and serious acting work in the film either, but to their credit, I think they do well in that few minutes they got. The previous one is a bit dull in the character of the bored, somewhat neutral rich wife, while the latter play the character of a middle-aged European millionaire who is loaded with money and a little tired of the ordinary behavior of women, - and perhaps too indulgent with his wife, Amber - and I think that Greenwood does it relatively well as Ritche expected it from him.

In any case, while the original work brought world fame to the two protagonists, the remake was almost buried by viewers and critics worldwide. Of course, there could be many reasons for this, it would be unnecessary to go into it further, but in my opinion, all this bad-mouthing was unfounded, because the film did have positives. Starting with the beautiful images, the introduction of the flashy rich, then the twist and role reversal towards the middle of the film, it kept me in front of the screen the whole time. As a big fan of Ritchie, I might be a bit biased, but I admit that I was curious to see what would come out of this and I admit that I laughed a lot, there were jokes in it, especially in the first 40 minutes **(illustration 3k)**. I don't think the "abusive" parts should be taken too seriously either, let's face it, there is much more violence in today's comedies and perhaps also in love dramas than in films of a similar nature and genre back then. There is no doubt, however, that if Ritchie had directed it now, it is likely that there would be much more serious criticism and accusations for these scenes. By the way, the movie were shot by cinematographer Alex Barber, who was previously responsible for shooting several of Madonna's video clips. Swept Away was edited by Eddie Hamilton (,, Top Gun: Maverick"), and the soundtrack was mostly composed by Michel Colombier ("New Jack City").

Another interesting thing about the film is that the stunning shots were taken on the azure waters and white sandy beaches of Sardinia and Malta, in the fall of 2001, under increased safety standards, and really, the visuals speak for themselves. Swept Away is the film that is provides the viewer one of the best visual experience **(illustration 31)**.

I would conclude the presentation of the director's third feature film by saying that in fact, it wasn't so bad. There is no doubt that making such a big change after two such bombastic movies, both in terms of genre, pace, and everything else, is quite a bold move. But this also speaks to the courage of the director and shows that he is not afraid to try himself in something else, which may be completely new compared to like what he's used to, like what he's done up until that point. It has happened to others in a similar way, see M. Night Shyamalan, whose first films at the beginning of his career were also accompanied by ovations and cheers. Then the sharp change and the production of some other films, which differed from what he had been used to, suddenly made him the object of public loathing in the film world, and I would add that the ruthlessness of the critics helped a lot in this. This film was Guy Ritchie's best and most memorable direction? No. It could have been better? Maybe. Was it possible to have fun on it? By all means. Did this take anything away from his talent as a director and make the assessment of his previous works worse? Absolutely not. That he is indeed an excellent filmmaker, just as Shyamalan, G.R. proved again and again in his later films.

3a

3b

3c

3d

3e

3f

3g

3h

3i

3j

3k

31

Revolver (2005)

Roughly three years after the release of Swept Away, on September 22, 2005, Guy Ritchie released Revolver, a crime action drama he co-wrote with French filmmaker Luc Besson. With the Anglo-French cinema heavily imbued with Kabbalah, numerology and psychology, he somewhat returned to his roots, to the directorial style in which perhaps he is the best in the film world. Unlike his first two works, however, he chose somewhat darker mood, and certain religious elements and a deeper insight into the individual's psyche appear for the first time in his work. This film also received a mixed reception, but compared to his previous directorial, people liked this thought-provoking and brilliantly photographed twisted philosophical lesson much more, and Ritchie's loyal fans outright exalted it.

Considered almost a loose change in the film world, the movie, shot for about $85,000, didn't bleed at the box office either, and to date has generated about $7 million for the Revolver Pictures Limited, Toff Guy Films, and TPS Star production companies. Thanks to the production activities of Luc Besson *("The Fifth Element")* and his wife, Virginie Silla *("Lucy")*, the French influence is also strongly felt in the film. It's perfectly fit with Ritchie's marks, who can pour English mafia stories into such an elegant form which we can see in this work also. While both *"Lock"* and *"Snatch"* demanded more thorough attention from the viewer, Revolver is even more complex than them and I dare to say that multiple viewings are recommended for those who want to understand everything, if it's possible at all, due to the nature and structure of the film.

It is unprecedented and unique in film history for a gangster story to be in a religious and psychological framework in such an enjoyable way. It is true that Guy's fourth work and third "tough guy" movie bears some similarities to several cult films, such as *"Fight Club"* (especially regarding the ending), but it can definitely be considered unique **(illustration 4a)**. In terms of its central theme, even if at the beginning it is seems like an other film that based on a character released from prison - who makes his life's goal to punish the one who sent him there - it soon becomes clear that it is much more than that and it will be something completely different at this time **(illustration 4b)**. Of course, this required not only the director's completely new approach to the subject, but also the excellent acting of Jason Statham - who played the main character, the well-known gambler and tricky card player in the underworld, Jake Green -, who now works with Ritchie for the third time.

People rightly compare Revolver to this day mainly with *"Snatch"* and not only because of the similarity in style and genre. Both when Snatch came out and when Revolver was released, there were high expectations for the director, and this is usually always the case if somebody brought something to the table before. Here, however, Ritchie may have had an even more difficult task, because after the negative reception of *"Swept Away"* it is not certain that his career would have survived another failure. However, he managed to avoid this and made one of the most enjoyable films of 2005 for us.

What makes it different from *"Lock"* and *"Snatch"* is that it only has one main character and the whole story is based on him. Jake Green, in possession of a mysterious trick, previously triumphant at many poker tables, now after 7 years in solitary confinement **(illustration 4c)** he wants to take revenge on the local casino owner and mob boss, Macha (Ray Liotta - *"Goodfellas"*), who - in the film it's not entirely clear why exactly - get him behind bars **(illustration 4d)**. The story is partly about the fight between the two, and partly about Jake - or as his two helpers, Zach (Vincent Pastore – *„Big Pussy"* from *"Sopranos"*) and Avi (Andree 3000 - rap group *"Outcast"*) call him, Mr. Green - and about his internal struggles, the movie moves forward by presenting the complicated chain of events that befall him **(illustration 4e)**.

Although even summarizing the story itself is a serious challenge (it must have been difficult to write it...), everyone can notice that most of the characters in the film have an impact on the events. Everything and everyone is connected to each other, both the main plot and from the point of view of the conclusion of the film. Be Macha's favorite hitman, who looks like an introverted librarian, played by the excellent British actor Mark Strong *("Kingsman"* films) **(illustration 4f)** or the Welsh-born Andrew Howard *("Limitless")* who plays Jake's brother Billy). It seems that everyone is in the right place in their roles, as we were used to from Guy Ritchie films **(illustration 4g)**. The dialogues are excellent this time as well, the narration perfectly supports the visual world built with particular sophistication and intelligence and does not allow you to get lost even in the midst of the many action-packed scenes. Time, as we have seen in Ritchie's earlier and later films, is not strictly linear here either, but from the point of view of understanding the story, it has to be like that.

As Jason Statham progresses in his career, his acting is getting noticeably better and with this film he proved that he is also excellent at portraying more complex characters and last but not least, according to many, even hair looked good on him. Ray Liotta (Rest in Peace) was also a good choice for the role of the gang leader, who is not always sure of himself, sickly suspicious and a regular solarium visitor, so he is seen in minimal clothing in about half of his scenes. Both Vincent Pastore and Andre Benjamin (Andre 3000) excellently took on the skin of the cold, self-righteous, determined and unscrupulous usurer-thief underworld characters **(illustration 4h)**.

Although the critics had a sharp opinion about the 1 hour and 51 minute philosophical crime drama and tried to drag it down as much as possible, they agreed that despite all its faults, it is a demanding work. Their main problem was that sometimes the story management, which switches to a slow pace, does not really go anywhere, and that it did not provide the same pleasure as the two previous crime films of a similar caliber.

In my opinion, the movie didn't deserve most of the criticism it received. There is no doubt that after two such big guns and a completely different type of work, trying to return to our genre again by put something new into the ingredients - so that the taste is similar, but still a little different - can be a particularly big challenge. But a world class a director like Guy Ritchie, accomplished the goal he set himself well and also selected the team of contributors excellently, with the help of whom they put together a great work. The visual pleasures are partially attributed to the cinematographer Tim Maurice-Jones, and partially to the editors, named Romesh Aluwihare *("As If")*, Ian Differ *("Alien vs. Predator")* and James Herbert *("Edge of Tomorrow")*. Without exception, all the songs in the film were composed by composer Nathaniel Méchaly *("Taken"* films) with the help of drummer Maxime Garoute *("Tell No One!")*.

The film's positives include, among other things, that it is characterized by extremely dynamic storytelling, does not let you wander while watching it and really makes you think, in addition to the fact that we can see great acting, and the overall visual experience and musical effect are truly excellent. Anyone who likes puzzle movies or those that make you think about what happened for hours (or even days) afterwards will definitely like it. There are traces of Guy Ritchie's hands on it, and we can simultaneously see it as an action film that entertains the masses, with a slightly more complicated story than usual. And at the same time, we can think of it as a cult film made for a narrow group in the middle of the 2000s. There is no doubt that it is not made for everyone and it requires a good amount of openness, but if you have it, then anyone can enjoy it, as long as they find the fun parts in it. It is worth looking for the revised version, as the film was released in two versions, the latter of which was screened in some American cinemas in December 2007.

I would like to end this chapter by saying that although I really liked Revolver (I saw it for the first time more than 10 years ago and I just watched it again) - and you can almost find fault in it with a magnifying glass -, I think that Ritchie has directed even better films plenty both before and after the film. However, what makes the cinema stand out from the other G.R. films, is the character of teaching. Already at the beginning of the film, the quotations that appear (I really like quotations) warn us to pay close attention, because now there will be something to think about. The thoughts of the professors and teachers speaking at the end of the film prove to be a great conclusion, they can also be understood as a kind of summary, which are meant to support and adequately interpret the conclusion of the film **(illustration 4i)**. Of these, the last is perhaps the most expressive of all.

To quote former President of the Philosophical Research Society Dr. Obadiah S. Harris, Ph.D.:

"Our biggest enemy is our own inner perception, our ego. Our own ego."

4a

4b

4c

4d

4e

4f

4g

4h

4i

RocknRolla (2008)

Just like *"Revolver"*, the director's fifth feature film was released 3 years after the production and presentation of the previous one. This was the RocknRolla, a 2008 British-French-American action thriller which made with some mob and crime feeling. After the romantic comedy in 2002 and then the philosophical action drama in 2005, it can be said that Guy Ritchie turned back to the path he started with *"Lock"* and then continued with *"Snatch"*.

Just like for all his previous works, he also wrote the screenplay for RocknRolla, and for the first time in his life he also tried his hand as a producer, furthermore Joel Silver *("Die Hard", "Matrix")*, Steve Clark-Hall and Susan Downey *("Sherlock Holmes")* also played a major role in the production of the film. As with his previous crime films, the footage was mostly shot in London on interior locations, with only a few scenes set in exterior areas such as tennis and golf courses, and two cuts were shot in Stoke Park, Buckinghamshire **(illustration 5a)**.

Ritchie announced his new film back in May 2007, then he started casting in June and the camera started rolling on the 19th of the same month.

What is New York for Woody Allen and Philadelphia for M. Night Shyamalan, seems to be London for Guy Ritchie, as many of his films are set and filmed here. The 1 hour and 54 minute underworld action crime film - which also contains many funny scenes thanks to the excellent dialogues -, was first shown in UK cinemas on September 5, 2008 and immediately became a huge audience favorite.

The story takes place entirely in the British capital and among others focuses on dubious real estate transactions, the theft of a very valuable painting, an amateur London robbery gang, Russian mobsters, a pretty accountant, and a drug-addicted ex-rock star. Just as with *"Lock"* and *"Snatch"*, it would be a bit difficult to determine exactly who the main character of the film is. The perfect casting and the amazing acting work of many actors allows us to conclude that the director does not wanted to highlight one or two people, not like in the case of *"Swept Away"* or *"Revolver"*. And this time too it can be felt that most of the characters presented are all equally important from the point of view of the story. At the beginning, we can believe that the main character is Lenny, who sees himself several times as the king of London - played by the recently deceased Tom Wilkinson *("Michael Clayton")* - he is in the center of the plot **(illustration 5b)**. Then One-Two appears, played by Gerard Butler *("300")*, on whom not only the camera focuses, but also the story, which really starts at about 20 minutes **(illustration 5c)**. Meanwhile, the young Tom Hardy *("Mad Max", "Venom"* films*)* playing Bob appears, and for a moment it seems that he will be the central figure **(illustration 5d)**.

With the central object, however, the situation is already clearer, the previously mentioned high-value painting, initially lent out of goodwill and later stolen, will be the one represented by the rifles in *"Lock"* and the diamond in *"Snatch"* **(illustration 5e)**. While in *"Swept Away"* not an object is the matter, but the question of whether love will develop between the two people with radically different personalities, however in *"Revolver"* everyone is curious about the mysterious Mr. Gold. It seems that for Ritchie this kind of centralization, when he weaves the events around either an object or a question (idea) or a mysterious person, has worked so far and works very well, because this kind of line management provides a great support and foundation for his films and it also includes them in a kind of framework, it gives them a great basis of comparison, which keeps the often rambling plot under control.

As I mentioned before, at the center of the story is essentially a painting, which is a symbol of the sealing of an agreement between Lenny - a well-known figure of the London underworld -, and a same type notorious Russian businessman Uri (Karel Roden - *"The Bourne Supremacy"*). The latter lends the picture to Lenny, until he settle his debt **(illustration 5f)**. The picture is especially important to the Russian, he sees it as a mascot, according to him, it has brought him luck so far and, of course, later he would like to get it back from Lenny. The trouble starts when someone steals this piece of art from Lenny's office, and when One-Two (Butler) and his partner Mumbles (Idris Elba - *"Wire"*) **(illustration 5g)** also steal the Russian's money he intended for Lenny. That's when the real action and the mad chase begin, interests collide, deals fail and new antagonisms emerge between the underworld figures appears in the film. In the midst of the complications, we get to know Lenny's son, the narcissistic drug addict ex-rock musician Johnny Quid (Toby Kebbel - *"Servant"*) **(illustration 5h)**, and this is when the charming accountant, the mysterious Stella comes into play (Thandie Newton – *"Westworld"*) **(illustration 5i)**. Another important character is Lenny's right-hand man, Archie (Mark Strong - *"Kingsman"*), who has nothing more important thing to do than to retrieve the painting **(illustration 5j)**.

Of course, it goes without saying that in the midst of the events, we can once again witness many forms of violence, from threats to retaliation, but we can also see in this film well and less well-executed robberies, furthermore sophisticated interrogations and several fight scenes and a lot of gunshots too. Just the way Guy Ritchie movies usually present it in a highly entertaining way. In addition, there are plenty of funny moments, a dance scene reminiscent of the *"Pulp Fiction"* **(illustration 5k)**, a crazy chase and many more humorous parts.

The fact that these scenes really turned out to be so enjoyable can be thanks for the harmony between the director and the actors who provide exceptional performances. Ritchie (and his casting staff) not only did a very good job while choosing the actors, but he also excelled in directing them, so that each of them brilliantly fulfilled the task of shaping the character assigned to him/her. Both Gerard Butler, Tom Hardy and Idris Elba, as well as Toby Kebbel, who was still less known around the world at the time (who has been one of my favorites since *"Servant"*), Thandie Newton and Mark Strong play excellent roles. In addition to them, even actors like Chris Bridges (rapper Ludacris - *"Fast and Furious"* films) and Jeremy Piven *("Entourage")* **(illustration 5l)** add color to the film. And Tom Wilkinson is downright brilliant, alongside the three robber friends, one of, if not the most funny character in the film.

Although the reviews of the film were quite mixed, overall they were more positive than negative. This happened partly because, according to the majority of critics, Ritchie started to return to the right direction with this film and find his own style, his own roots. They also stated that although this movie does not invent anything new and the idea is not very original, furthermore the first hour passes relatively slowly, the performances of actors such as Gerard Butler, Mark Strong or Toby Kebbel still make it unforgettable this production. Chris Tilly from IGN UK, for example, stated that RocknRolla is an adrenaline-pumping thriller-comedy that is witty and exciting from start to finish and gave the film 4 out of 5 maximum points.[3]

RocknRolla, which was made for 18 million dollars and brought in nearly 26 million dollars worldwide, was shot by cinematographer David Higgs and, like *"Revolver"*, it was also edited by James Herbert. Steve Isles was responsible for the film score, which, although also dynamic, is perhaps somewhat toned down from *"Snatch"* and less colorful and diverse in terms of genres.

---

[3] https://www.ign.com/articles/2008/09/02/rocknrolla-uk-review

RocknRolla was produced by the director's own company, Toff Guy, with the participation of Joel Silver's Dark Castle Entertainment and with the French Studio Canal. At the time of the film's release, Ritchie stated that if the film receives good reviews and is seen by many people, then he will start thinking more seriously about a possible second and third part. According to some unconfirmed information, he has already written the script for the second part, in which Johnny, Archie and quite a few other characters would return, and the title of the films would be *"The Real RocknRolla"*, and *"RocknRolla Suicide"*.

Richie's complicated but all the more exciting script mixes diverse and unique characters into even more diverse and impossible situations, and then everything falls into place at the end of the production, so the viewer experiences a sense of completeness about the film after the nearly two hours of entertainment everyone can get up from your chair without a sense of absence and with satisfaction. It can be said that with this film, Guy Ritchie returned to the previously traveled path and the track he had beaten for himself, as well as to directing successful and audience favorite films. And how true this is, he will be showing then in his later works too, right after RocknRolla, in the first act of a sequel movie, in the best film adaptation of a well-known detective story to date.

5a

5b

5c

5d

5e

5f

5g

5h

5i

5j

5k

5l

Sherlock Holmes (2009)

The 10th anniversary of the beginning of his career, the year 2009 proved to be particularly successful for the British filmmaker father of five. In December of that year, the most success film adaptation of a detective story in the history of cinemas, the story of Sherlock Holmes was shown. This time, the main producers of the mystical action-adventure film made in American-German co-production were Joel Silver and Susan Downey - the wife of the protagonist Robert Downey Jr. -, as well as Dan Lin *("Lego films")* and Lionel Wigram (*"Harry Potter"* films). From a story by the latter and Michael Robert Johnson *("Pompeii")*, the screenplay was also written by Johnson, along with Anthony Peckham *("Don't Say a Word")* and Simon Kinberg *("The Martian," "355")*.

It was a bold undertaking by Ritchie, re-adapting the story of Holmes, because turning a novel into a film is always a difficult task and, as we know, comparisons with previous adaptations always happen in such films. In this regard, Ritchie has successfully overcome the obstacles, as the majority of viewers consider the film to be the most entertaining adaptation of Holmes to this day. Filming began in October 2008 and the work took place mostly in the north of Manchester, as well as in Liverpool, Wapping, located on the Thames and on its north bank, but we can see, for example, a shipyard, a port or the Tower Bridge under construction **(illustration 6a)**. The crew also worked on locations such as London's Fulham Road and Brompton Cemetery, but also filmed scenes in the Freemason's Hall and St. Paul's Cathedral **(illustration 6b)**.

The eccentric private investigator from Sir Arthur Conan Doyle's novel is played by Robert Downey Jr. *("Iron man" and "Avengers")*, while his partner Dr. John Watson is played by Jude Law *("Cold Mountain", "Holiday")* **(illustration 6c)**. The main female role was given to Rachel Mcadams, she portrays Irene Adler, the professional thief, who, according to the story, was previously Holmes's lover **(illustration 6d)**. In addition to them, Mark Strong also appears as Lord Henry Blackwood, who likes to practice black magic, and has now played in a Guy Ritchie film for the third time in a row **(illustration 6e)**.

The film had its premiere in London on December 14, 2009, and then on Christmas, December 25, it was shown across America, and from the 26th in the United Kingdom and Ireland. From the first earnings figures, it was clear that the $90 million budget film would be a huge success, and it was Ritchie's highest-grossing film until Aladdin. In America alone, it opened with more than $62 million in its first weekend, finishing second behind the first part of Avatar. The detective story with a playing time of 2 hours and 8 minutes, although evoking a period atmosphere, but novel in terms of its characters, broke the one-day Christmas record and also produced good numbers later on, bringing in 524 million dollars worldwide for Warner Bros, Village Roadshow and Silver Pictures.

Set in Victorian London at the end of the 19th century **(illustration 6f)**, the story really begins when Holmes and Watson are commissioned (almost obliged) by Scotland Yard to cooperate with them in the investigation of an unusual mystery and an extremely sensitive case (for the authorities) in its solution **(illustration 6g)**. The satanist Lord Blackwood, who had already been captured for his crimes, handed over to the hands of the law, hanged and then buried -according to all indications -, has returned from the afterlife, as he has left his grave **(illustration 6h)**. The two detectives have to find out if this is a supernatural occurrence or if there is a reasonable explanation for it.

In the role of Holmes, Robert Downey Jr. almost shines. In a very lifelike and particularly entertaining way, he takes on the role of a detective who, according to Watson, is rather bohemian, scattered, and who sometimes does not like to follow social norms. In the film, Sherlock is an enthusiastic practitioner of martial arts, occasionally participates in illegal boxing matches, regularly experiments on his own dog, does not leave his Baker Street home, which is darkened even during the day, for months, does not disdain various drugs and does not really like company. Although the stag beetle headgear does not appear here - unlike most depictions of Holmes - the pipe remains, and his attire now resembles that of an artist or poet. Despite all this, the character is a brilliant mind - as in Doyle's works, in the film as well -, who investigates very thoroughly and solves complex criminal cases with extreme care, the evidence of which is often revealed at the last moment, while of course he does not shy away from being a real showman, often in a theatrical manner presents his explanation of the solutions to the cases to the stakeholders **(illustration 6i)**.

Jude Law also plays the role of Dr. Watson very well, he plays similarly well the young and fresh doctor, who, due to Holmes's debauchery and harmful, self-destructive lifestyle, he has to become more serious and responsible for his age. But at the same time he is very intelligent and loyal, as well as an exceedingly patient co-detective, who sometimes has to bring to heel his partner **(illustration 6j)**. The chemistry and harmony between the two is excellent, which makes the film even more lovable, thanks to these two great actors. In many cases, they are opposites of each other, especially when we look at their private lives, but when it comes to crime cases, they support and help each other in order to find a solution. Mark Strong is also exceptionally good in portraying the dark and cold Blackwood, and Eddie Marsan also provides adequate acting support in the role of the determined Inspector Lestrade, who cannot do without Holmes' help **(illustration 6k)**. Rachel McAdams *("The Notebook")* is very lovable in the character of Irene, the charming and sensual, but even more refined thief, who gives the appearance of a nice classy lady **(illustration 6l)**. Who is also worth highlighting is Kelly Reilly *("Pride and Prejudice")*, who plays Dr Watson's lover, Mary Morstan, the lovely English lady whom the doctor wants to propose to as soon as possible **(illustration 6m)**.

The film received generally positive reviews. However, there were some negative opinions regarding some action scenes that are not very relevant to the story, such as saving Irene in the factory building. Also, some complained about the excessive special effects and that the director's detective was quite different from Basil

Rathbone and Nigel Bruce's Holmes and Watson. Others objected that the writers changed the story of how Holmes and Mary met, because in the original work the woman was a former client of the detective.

The movie was nominated for and won several awards, including the Golden Globe Award for Best Actor and the Irish Film and Television Award, which Robert Downey Jr. was proud to receive for his portrayal of the eccentric and clownish detective, who is absolutely not free from irony. This is also proof that the refreshing and rethinking of the character of Holmes was successful and the risk-taking also worked. Put him into a new form, the numerous tricks and CGI, and of course the engaging play of the actors managed to make him even more lovable to the audience.

The music of the film was composed by one of Hollywood's busiest musical talents, the famous German-born composer Hans Zimmer *("True Romance", "Dune", "The Creator")*, who was also nominated an Oscar for his work in 2010 in the Best Original Score category. Zimmer bought an out-of-tune piano for just $200 and used it throughout the film's orchestration process, creating an exceptional musical atmosphere for the movie. In this way, he was able to give the film a funny, but at the same time spooky atmosphere, which fits perfectly with the new Holmes character brought to life by Downey.

The beautiful footage praises the handiwork of the French-born cinematographer Philipe Rousselot *("A River Runs Through It", "Interview with the Vampire")*, whose images were also edited by James Herbert, who worked with the director for the third time. Particularly pleasing are the battle scenes that are preceded by calculations, these are extremely imaginative sequences, typically ones that we still remember in connection with the film years later **(illustration 6n)**. To smuggle in some comparison between the lines, the slow sequences of brilliantly structured fistfights, the repeated pauses reminded me a bit of the boxing scenes of "Snatch", but of course in a good way and reminded me of the recently seen knock outs, performed by "One punch" Mickey which are by far my favorite fighting scenes among the thousands of movies I've ever seen.

Contemporary London is beautiful and the shots have a magical atmosphere. We are almost there on the sometimes muddy, sometimes cobbled streets, in the middle of the rushing stream of people, in the company of market hawkers, beggars, pickpockets, gypsy women who tell fortunes, pleasure girls and the few wealthy financiers

(illustration 6o). The acting is excellent, the visuals are perfectly executed, the story is exciting, and the atmosphere creates a good feeling. The film remains faithful to the style of the author's original stories. Slightly different, but not too much from the portrayal of character of the original work, but at the same time it's completely innovative and cleverly executed. Fans of the novel can be glad that Ritchie took the director's chair this time, as she made a truly enjoyable movie out of Doyle's great literary masterpiece. The 2009 Sherlock Holmes also received another Oscar nomination, namely in the category of best visual design, which unfortunately it did not manage to turn into a statue, but it has received the award of the Art Director Guild in the same category, as well as the recognition of the best thriller of the Empire Award.

Guy Ritchie's sixth direction and first novel adaptation is perfect entertainment for anyone who likes thought-provoking, sometimes slower-paced, sometimes more action-packed movies, interspersed with great dialogue and funny scenes, excellently photographed and orchestrated.

6a

6b

6c

6d

6e

6f

6g

6h

6i

6j

6k

6l

6m

6n

6o

Sherlock Holmes: A Game of Shadows (2011)

The seventh film directed by Guy Ritchie and his first film that can be considered a sequel was the 2011 film Sherlock Holmes: A Game of Shadows. After the great success of the first part in 2009, there was no question that it was only a matter of time and a sequel will come. According to some unconfirmed reports, the film was heavily influenced by Sir Conan Doyle's short story „The Final Problem". The main producers of the mysterious action-adventure film were once again Susan Downey, Dan Lin, Joel Silver and Lionel Wigram, and the script was written by the writer couple, Kieran and his wife Michele Mulroney ("Power Rangers").

In October 2010, several people witnessed Robert Downey Jr. and Jude Law rehearsing a fight scene in Richmond Park. Later that month, Warner Bros, Village Roadshow Pictures and Silver Pictures rented a 1946 steamer PS Waverly to film on the La Manche Channel, and in mid-November, a green backdrop (chroma keying) were set up at Didcot Railway Centre - which is often used in movies -, when they were shooting a big action scene. In addition to it the film's locations also were the

Strasbourg Cathedral, the Victoria Bridge in Worcestershire, the Hampton Palace in London and the Oxford University **(illustration 7a)**.

The two central characters, i.e. Holmes and Watson, were played again by Robert Downey Jr. and Jude Law **(illustration 7b)**, but the female protagonist this time was Noomi Rapace *("Prometheus")*, she played Madame Simza, the mysterious and gypsy woman who can fight pretty well **(illustration 7c)**. Alongside to her, another important female figure appears again, namely Irine Adler, whom we could met at the first part, who was also played by Rachel McAdams, although she had a much smaller role in this film **(illustration 7d)**. And in the role of the negative protagonist, appears on the screen Jared Harris *("Chernobyl")*, who brought Professor James Moriarty to life and showed a brilliant performance **(illustration 7e)**.

The Game of Shadows takes place one year after the first part, and the film may seem like a direct continuation of the first movie, but the situation is not that simple and clear. According to the filmmakers, they had in mind all along that the film should be able to pay it's way alone and not depend too much on the previous one, and that it should not be a prerequisite for understanding it.

Presumably that's why it wasn't given the title Sherlock Holmes 2 either, although it is said that this was the first idea in the beginning.

So the film begins roughly where the first part left off, when Holmes tracks down Professor Moriarty, whom they considers responsible for numerous bombings carried out across Europe, claiming many lives. Furthermore, even Irine plays an important role in Holmes' pursuit of his new arch-enemy, whose subsequent absence can be felt throughout the rest of the film mainly due to the chemistry between Holmes and her. In the search for the terrorist villain and then in thwarting his evil plans, his number one helper is Doctor Watson again, as well as a mysterious gypsy woman, Simza, who joins them and participates in the dangerous mission. During the adventures, we get to know Sherlock's older brother, the measured and constantly teasing Mycroft, played by the writer, producer and actor Stephen Fry *("V for Vendetta")* **(illustration 7f)**. In addition, Mary, whom Watson met in the first part, also appears - whom Watson finally marries here - she is the same charming and full-hearted woman as in the first part - although she does not know what she has undertaken -, now as the detective's wife, she will have much more excitement and trials.

After a funny wedding - which brings a special color to the film - she immediately gets into the thick of events, even though she only wanted a beautiful and memorable honeymoon, which, if not beautiful, will definitely be memorable for her **(illustration 7g)**. Watson was almost thinking of retirement, but he decided to do one last joint work with Holmes, and then as a newlywed he found himself faced with one of the most dangerous and trying - but also extremely patriotic - challenges of his life. The stakes are huge, to prevent the mad professor from continuing his rampage, which Moriarty can use to trigger the outbreak of a worldwide conflict, namely World War I.

The two central characters are once again played with great experience and skill by Robert Downey Jr. and Jude Law, it's good to watch them as they really feel good in their roles and as they complement each other, they once again made a perfect couple. Noomi Rapace was also a good choice for the role of Simza, the character she brings, her appearance and style fit perfectly with the era. Stephen Fry's performance is also authentic and entertaining as Holmes' older brother, I think that this is how you can play the role of an older sibling with high-hat, who even calls his adult younger brother by his nickname (I know how it feels, I have an older brother too…). And Jared Harris is

Moriarty himself, as if he had been preparing for this role all his life, is an absolutely believable antagonist, big congratulations to both the casting and the director, it was a magnificent choice. His composure and the emission of his intellect, mixed with the fact that he's actually a vile and very dangerous villain, make for a pretty terrifying mixture. The way he tells Holmes with an unblinking face at their first meeting to prepare, because he has never dealt with such an enemy before, is one of the central scenes of the film, which evokes serious emotions in the viewer **(illustration 7h)**.

Just like the first part, The Game of Shadow received positive reviews overall and critics praised the acting of Downey and Law, as well as Jared Harris, in addition to the action scenes. The negative opinions mostly related to the absence of Irine, i.e. Miss McAdams, who - according to the majority - Rapace could not replace, as well as the fact that the potential of this character was not used, even though it would have been possible. Starting with the emotional thread, to the personality development of the charming but twisted thief. Others objected that the excessive use of speeding up and then slowing down in the action scenes is becoming boring. It feels as if the director does this in his films for sheer fun, not because it is one of his trademarks and because he wants to emphasize that way the certain scenes. Whether this is true or not is up to everyone to decide for themselves.

Comparing the two films, it can be stated that while the first part was somewhat slower, the second does not stop for a moment and is much more lively than its predecessor. In terms of what it has to say and its atmosphere, it goes less deep, but it also has plenty of mystery and a dark tone. The first film wasn't particularly slow either, but the Game of Shadow is a different competition and the characters are in constant motion, among other things, because that's the only way they can survive and the plot moves forward in this way. The action complemented and made more entertaining by, among other things, the inventive humor and by excellent jokes (see Stanley the old butler, whose real life name is also this**) (illustration 7i).**

Just like for the first part, Hans Zimmer provided the outstanding musical accompaniment to this film too. In addition to the works of great composers such as Mozart, Strauss, Schubert or even Ennio Morricone, he also included authentic gypsy music in the film's musical score. He relied heavily on the violin and accordion, and listened to local musicians from many European countries, then worked with them to make the whole selection as authentic and lifelike as possible. He went with the director among others to Italy, France and Slovakia, to search for the genres and compositions on which he composed his own frenetic music for the movie.

Taking place in beautiful landscapes and prestigious buildings, the movie, which is more action-packed than the previous part, was recorded by Philippe Rousselot, as in the first part, and the frames were also edited by the editor James Herbert. Thus the audience could get an another extremely enjoyable, this time 2 hours and 9 minutes long Guy Ritchie film with impressive visuals **(illustration 7j)**.

The creators also planned the release of the Game of Shadow for the end of the year and around Christmas. It was released in cinemas in the United States and the United Kingdom on December 16, 2011, and in most countries, viewers could see it from the 25th of the same month. The movie was just as big a success and earned somewhat more worldwide than the first part - 543 million dollars - but it also cost more to make - about 125 million. While the first part was in 8th place, Shadow Game is earned also a nice 12th place, in the list of the highest-grossing films of 2011.

The director continued the unique atmosphere that he started in the first part and it can be said, improved it. More action, more bullets and explosions, more slow motion, more intellectual content, more supporting role and of course a lot more jokes **(illustration 7k)**. Again, excellent acting, great sets and lighting, elegant late 1800s costumes, period vehicles and props, and an exciting plot with multiple reference to real history, to name a few of the many positives **(illustration 7l)**.

If you liked the first part, it is definitely recommended, but if you haven't seen it, you can watch it without a further ado. Great fun is guaranteed and after that you might even get the urge also to start the first act on a gloomy autumn evening.

7a

7b

7c

7d

7e

7f

7g

7h

7i

7j

7k

7l

The Man from U.N.C.L.E (2015)

After an absence of nearly 4 years, in the summer of 2015, the director, who holds a black belt in Brazilian jiu jitsu, presented his 8th film, a spy movie titled The Man from U.N.C.L.E. Ritchie also wrote the screenplay for the work, classified by IMDB as an action, adventure and comedy genre, together with Lionel Wigram, and they also wrote the story together with David C. Wilson *("Supernova")* and Jeff *Kleeman ("Frankeinstein", " The judge")*. The main producers of the film were also Ritchie and Wigram, as well as Steve Clark-Hall and John Davis *("Waterworld", "I, Robot")*. The makers of the film were Wigram Productions, RatPac-Dune Entertainment and Davis Entertainment, as well as Warner Bros. Pictures, and the latter is also its main distributor to this day.

The Man from U.N.C.L.E. is based on the 1964 MGM television series of the same title, many episodes of which were produced by Norman Felton *("Studio One '57")* and Sam Rolfe *("Killjoy '81")*, and the Turner Entertainment Co., which is the producer and owner of the original episodes, also participated making the film. Ritchie began directing the film on September 9, 2013 with cinematographer John Mathieson *("Gladiator")*, editor

James Herbert and his crew in the United Kingdom, then in Italy and the camera also rolled in locations such as London's Royal Victoria Docks or the Regent's Park **(illustration 8a)**. And the memorable car chase in East Berlin during the first act was filmed at Chatham Historic Dockyard in Kent **(illustration 8b)**.

The story of the 60s spy film takes place at the height of the Cold War, when one of the CIA's best men, Napoleon Solo (Henry Cavill - *"Man of Steel"*), who used to spend his days as a painting thief **(illustration 8c)**, is forced to enter into an alliance of interests with the KGB as well with one of their best-trained agents, the intelligence soldier Illya Kuryakin (Armie Hammer - *"The Lone Ranger")*, who very determined and loyal to his nation until death **(illustration 8d)**. The stakes are huge, they have to save the world from the crazy underworld criminal organization ruled by the multi-millionaire couple and from their soon-to-be-done nuclear bomb . Alexander (Luca Calvani - *"When in Rome"*) **(illustration 8e)** and Victoria Vinciguerra (Elizabeth Debiczki - *"The Crown"*) **(illustration 8f)** probably kidnapped the Nazi scientist Udo Teller (Christian Berkel - *"Valkyrie"*) **(illustration 8g)** to make a weapon of mass destruction for them. He used to work for the Americans and he has a daughter, the charming German car mechanic Gaby Teller. The newly allied agents therefore seek out Gaby (Alicia Vikander - *"Tomb Raider"*) **(illustration 8h)** so that she can help them find her long-lost father, who is presumably kidnapped by his brother Uncle Rudi (Sylvester Groth - *"Inglourious Basterds"*) and handed him over to the couple **(illustration 8i)**.

The premiere of the film took place on August 2, 2015 in Barcelona, and from August 13 it was already available in countries such as Germany, Australia and Russia, and from the 14th it was shown in American and British cinemas.

I feel it's worth sharing some information about the background to the making of The Man from U.N.C.L.E., because it was a relatively long process before the day in March 2013 when Ritchie took on the direction of the film and re-signed to Warner. Producer John Davis acquired the rights to the original series 64 back in 1993 - 20 years before the film was made -, and then made an agreement to produce an adaptation with one of the TV show's co-producers, Norman Felton and with Warner. The project has been on the desks of many screenwriters and directors over the years, Steven Soderbergh, Matthew Vaughn and even Quentin Tarantino himself were discussed in connection with the direction, the latter for example, chose „*Jackie Brown*" instead of T.M.F.U. The start of the work was greatly hindered and stalled by the constant rewriting of the script and disagreements between the directors and the studio, which on occasion meant different views on the production costs of the film.

The situation regarding the selection of the final actors was not easy either. Tom Cruise was reportedly in talks to play Napoleon Solo, but due to his commitments with „*Mission Impossible - Rogue Nation*", his participation in the film did not materialize. In addition to Cruise, George Clooney also showed interest in playing the character, but according to the news, he could not take on the role of the CIA agent with a dubious past due to his recurring back pain. The producers considered, among others, Matt Damon, Ewan McGregor, Ryan Gosling, Channing Tatum, and even Leonardo Dicaprio to portray the womanizing spy. Before the selection of Swedish actress Alicia Vikander, Emily Blunt was originally supposed to play Gaby, but she also left the production after Steven Soderbergh's exit.

The casting was successful in the end and I think everyone will agree that the actors played their roles very well, especially the three main characters. The two men have a strong chemistry, but with the participation of the woman, the dominance of the three of them is even more evident, and in retrospect, they prove to be a perfect choice. The healthy masculine competition of Henry Cavill's Bond-like self-confidence and Armie Hammer's somewhat more serious, but at the same time soft-hearted, purposeful and principled characters, -Napoleon and Illya -, is perfectly offset by Alicia Vikander's sometimes feminine charm, other times her girlish emission and childish playfulness **(illustration 8j)**. What is particularly interesting about their performance is that the actors do not use their own accents. Cavill as a Brit is American, Hammer as an American is Russian, while Gaby as a Swede speaks with a German accent, for which they deserve special recognition. After getting to know the triumvirate, we gets the feeling that we would like to see them in many more episodes of, say, an exciting Netflix, HBO or any streaming services' series. Hugh Grant ("Notting Hill") also brings his usual thoroughness and intriguing monologues in the few moments in which he appears **(illustration 8k)** and Elizabeth Debiczki, who plays the main antagonist, also excels in the role of the wife, Victoria, who is just as evil and rampant as it is beautiful **(illustration 8l)**.

The film received mixed reviews, but viewers generally found it entertaining. Most of the negative feedback was generally about the confusion around the plot and some exaggerated action scenes and related to the end of the film. Of course, these were not such sharp criticisms and many reviewers emphasized that the faultless acting, the magnificent music, the many funny action scenes, the imaginative and well-written dialogues, - which, for example, perfectly matched the Russian accent -, made the film's flaws somewhat forgotten. On Metacritic the film received 56 out of 100 points based on the summation of 40 critics' opinions, which roughly means average reviews. The film's composer is Daniel Pemberton, who composed music for films such as *"The Counselor"*, *"Enola Holmes"* and *"Ferrari"*. The musical score received many positive reviews, in which the main role was played by classical instruments such as harpsichord, organ or flute, guitar and drums. The varied music creates a special atmosphere for the film and it evokes that era perfectly, the Cold War atmosphere, when the possibility of the next world-wide conflict was in the air.

The Man from U.N.C.L.E wasn't very profitable revenue-wise, earning only $110 million on a roughly $75 million budget. The reason for this is still a mystery, but maybe it had something to do with the fact that when the film was released, most people didn't really know where to "put it" and many couldn't connect it with the original show either, since it had been on the air for half a century.

And on the other hand, the episodes of this series are not available so easily, and the majority of cinema-goers in the summer of 2015 simply did not know it, including me. Neither the excellent direction, the exceptional acting, the historical aspect and the atmospheric music could not help the revenue data, but regardless, it can be stated that the majority of the viewers liked The Man from U.N.C.L.E., whose title stands for United Network Command for Law Enforcement. The film was also made into a 3D shooting action game for both IOS and Android operating system phones, entitled „*Mission: Berlin*", which is no longer available on either of them as of december 2018.

Another interesting fact about the 1 hour and 56 minute adaptation is that Rolling Stone magazine ranked the film 45th among the best action films of all time. I have always liked the subsequent explanation of the actions in the director's films, in which they interpret what happened (see *"Snatch", "Revolver", "RocknRolla", "Sherlock Holmes"*) this time this was no different and I think it is a great summary and conclusion of an entertaining action movie full of adventures and happenings where you also have to think a little **(illustration 8m)**. The director's usual slow-down-speed-up technique was left out of the film - which I missed a little -, but who knows if it would have fit to a film with such a story and atmosphere. In recent years, news of a possible sequel has also surfaced, according to which Mr. Wigram is already working on the second part at Hammer's suggestion, and Henry Cavill has also shown interest in playing Solo again. In any case, if that were the case, I'm sure that many fans, like me, would be happy to see these three beautiful people on the screen in another adventure **(illustration 8n)**. We hope the producers will consider it and if we have already received an another Sherlock, dear director, we would more than happy to see a similarly exciting story, enriched with colorful humorous action scenes, and beautifully photographed, an extremely atmospheric sequel.

8a

8b

8c

8d

8e

8f

8g

8h

8i

8j

8k

8l

8m

8n

King Arthur: Legend of the Sword (2017)

A little less than 2 years after the release of ,, *The Man from U.N.C.L.E. "*, on April 27, 2017, Mr. Ritchie's 9th film, the action-adventure drama called King Arthur: Legend of the Sword, premiere was held in select AMC theaters in the US at a certain King for a day event. Some say the film is fiction, while others say it's based on real British historical events.

Just like his previous film, the screenplay for this one was written together with Lionel Wigram, and Joby Harold *("Edge of Tomorrow")* also joined them during the work. In addition, the three of them are also the producers of the movie, and Steve Clark-Hall also took part in the production again, next to Akiva Goldsman *("A Beautiful Mind")* and Tory Tunnel *("Awake")*. They all had a major role in the making of the 2 hour 6 minute-long film that can also be partly classified as fantasy. After the two *"Sherlock"* movies and *"The Man from U.N.C.L.E."*, this was the 4th film in a row that the director directed for Warner Bros. Studio and the third that he made in the framework of working together with Village Road Show.

The film's screenplay, originally based on the story by Mr. Harold and David Dobkin *("The Judge")*, was inspired by the legends of King Arthur. According to the rumors, after *"King Arthur"* in 2004, the plans of the Warner Bros studio also included the production of new films related to the legends. One would have been the Excalibur, as well as a work based on the relationship between the king and Lancelot, or even the wizard. It was then that Ritchie came into the studio's sights, who had long wanted to direct a film about King Arthur.

"The Man from U.N.C.L.E" had not even been released in theaters when he began directing King Arthur in February 2015 and the camera started rolling in Windsor Great Park in the United Kingdom **(illustration 9a)**. Some scenes were shot in Snowdonia, North Wales **(illustration 9b)**, but the movie was also filmed around the villages of Shieldaig and Loch Torridon and on Bealach Applecross, Wester Ross, in the Scottish Highlands **(illustration 9c)**.

The story goes all the way back to the end of the 5th century and the beginning of the 6th century in Britain, when a kind and just king named Arthur lived in his court named Camelot. He is played in the film by the great British actor Charlie Hunnam extremely charismatically and by absolute experience **(illustration 9d)**. It is important to know about the myth that there is no specific and universally accepted story, which may establish the appropriateness of the claim that Arthur is a fictional person after all. Thus, many variations of the legend can be found in British literature, there have been many adaptations in theater productions, books and films, and the character of the king himself cannot be avoided at all. Generations have grown up on the stories and legends associated with Camelot, the brave and noble Lancelot and the wizard Merlin, and the many legends surrounding the magical sword Excalibur **(illustration 9e)**.

The plot of the present film begins in Arthur's infancy, when Arthur's father, Uther - played by Eric Bana *("Hulk")* with his usual professional acting - is determined to fight the evil wizard Mordred **(illustration 9f)**. The decisive deed, in terms of the progress of the story, on the other hand, is related to his brother Vortigern, who is played by Jude Law **(illustration 9g)**. It will be this act that will affect not only the child's life, but also the adult Arthur's life later on, and thus he will be who he is.

The film begins with an extremely busy and rich visual world, we fall into the middle of an action-packed battle scene that is more reminiscent of the last few minutes of a long adventure film, but despite its unusualness, this is an ingenious solution from the screenwriters and the director (who is partly, as we know in this case, is one and the same person) and these pictures are really entertaining, create curiosity in the viewer and at the same time command full attention. After that, the medieval heroic story - which also includes elements of comedy -, continues with a slightly slower story line. We can get to know the different stages of Arthur's young years, the stages of his maturation into a man **(illustration 9h)**.

We soon find ourselves at the plot that can be connected to Uther's previous act and Excalibur, and from here on the film becomes more eventful **(illustration 9i)** and the camera will really focus on the grown-up Arthur. Hunnam, who until then was best known to viewers as Jax from *"Sons of Anarchy"*, was chosen by the director for the main role in August 2014, and in September Ástrid Bergés-Frisbey was given the role of the mage *("Pirates of the Caribbean: On Stranger Tides")*. Originally, it was intended for Elizabeth Olsen, but in the end, the Spanish beauty got the role of the strange sorcerer, which she performed excellently well **(illustration 9j)**.

Djimon Hounsou, who exploded into the film world with the *"Blood Diamond"*, and Aiden Gillen, who is already well-known to everyone as "Littlefinger" in *"Game of*

Thrones", also did an above-average job to believably portray Arthur's helpers, Bedivere and Bill **(illustration 9k)**.

If we are talking about the casting, a special interesting thing in the film is that a famous British world-class football player also appears - slightly disguised -, who may not even recognize by some fans - I would not reveal his name -, furthermore the director also has a short cameo role and for the sake of the game, let's see if the dear reader can recognize them from the pictures **(illustration 9l)**. I think no one can deny that everyone is excellent and sparkles in the role assigned to them, but Jude Law is downright brilliant and gives one of the best performances of his life.

King Arthur: Legend of the Sword received average reviews and was generally not flooded with too many positive adjectives, but at the same time, viewers nor critics commented on it too badly neither. It is true that once again there were opinions - as before -, that Ritchie should rather return to gangster films inspired by the London underworld, such as the *"Lock"* and the *"Snatch"* or the *"RocknRolla"*, because he is the best in this. But in fact, overly negative reviews avoided Ritchie's Robin Hood-like Arthur - who is a thief, but also a hero who loves and protects his people. It can be said that after the screenings, people mostly had a positive opinion of both Ritchie and the film and considered it more of a fun spectacular action fantasy than a boring historical tale with costumes. It's true that it doesn't hurt to pay attention to the events and sometimes you need some patience with yourself until everything falls into place, but if you have that, you will definitely like this movie.

For example, film critic Peter Bradshaw wrote about the film for the Guardian:

"Guy Ritchie's cheerfully ridiculous Arthur is a gonzo monarch, a death-metal warrior-king. Ritchie's film is at all times over the top, crashing around its digital landscapes in all manner of berserkness, sometimes whooshing along, sometimes stuck in the odd narrative doldrum. But it is often surprisingly entertaining, and whatever clunkers he has delivered in the past, Ritchie again shows that a film-maker of his craft and energy commands attention, and part of his confidence in reviving King Arthur resides here in being so unselfconscious and unconcerned about the student canon that has gone before."

Despite the well-written script, the usual excellent work from Ritchie, the impressive acting, the CGI technique and the magical atmosphere, the movie failed at the box office. This was the first film of the director in his career, which generated less profit than it cost. Even the extra-high budget of 175 million dollars could not make the film a financial success, as only 149 million dollars have come back from it so far.

But, as we know, who likes good movies not decides whether it's good or not based on how much money it makes. I think it's a good movie, and I even dare to say that it's one of the best movies of 2017, as far as the story, the visuals, the excellent fight scenes and the acting concerned. It is therefore no coincidence that the film was nominated for many awards. This once again required John Mathieson's magical visuals, James Herbert's dynamic, eye-catching editing, and composer Daniel Pemberton's suspenseful sound effects, held together - like bricks in mortar -, by Ritchie's excellent direction. The flashback at the end of the film - which he had used several times before and still worked as well this time -, reminded me of the director's unique style, but the fast and slow transition of the images could not be found, but it wasn't missing from the film at all.

Anyone who understood and accepted Ritchie's previous films, along with their humor, visuals, structure, and unique style, is sure to sit down and watch this one with an open mind and will probably like it. Anyone who has not yet seen a work by the director will also benefit from being open-minded, and if you like fast-paced adventure films, it will contributes greatly in making this film memorable for them.

King Arthur: Legend of the Sword is an update of an old tale, its stylish presentation and packaging it in a new dress with the support of today's technical possibilities - in other words special effects - and the result speaks for itself. An excellent entertainment that satisfies all needs, which most people will definitely watch again a few years after the cinema experience.

In his next direction, Guy Ritchie also in his own style and this time conjured an old classic on the screen - namely for the first time in modern film history -, and this was none other than 2019's overwhelming blockbuster, Aladdin.

9a

9b

9c

9d

9e

9f

9g

9h

9i

9j

9k

91

Aladdin (2019)

The year 2019 was doubly successful for Guy Ritchie, as in May of that year, the cinemas showed his first film with a revenue exceeding 1 billion, Aladdin, and then roughly six months later, at the beginning of December, his gangster film „*The Gentlemen*". Disney's latest Aladdin, the family, adventure and comedy movie, is a remake and reimagining of the much-loved 1992 animated film. Many of us grew up on the best-known collection of „*1001 Arabian Nights*". One of the most famous of these is "*Aladdin and the Magic Lamp*", my parents also read it to me before going to bed when I was a child, just like from the "*Alibaba and 40 Thieves*" and "*The Adventures of Sinbad*" also. In addition to the book and the 1992 animated film starring Robin Williams, I also loved the Disney series based on this work, I always watched it on TV right after waking up on Saturday mornings, this is how the weekend started for me when I was in elementary school, pleasant memories are associated with this period. The film was directed by Ritchie, from a screenplay he co-wrote with John August *("Charlie and the Chocolate Factory")*. The extremely successful 2 hour 8 minute remake was produced by Dan Lin *("Sherlock" films)* and Jonathan Eirich *("Haunted Mansion")*.

The movie, which can easily be classified as a fantasy, romantic and film musical, was announced by Disney - which produced the film alongside Lin Pictures and Rideback - in October 2016, and then revealed the identity of the director - Ritchie - to the press. Principal photography began on 6 September 2017 at Longcross Studios in Surrey, England **(illustration 10a)** and concluded on 24 January 2018. The camera also rolled a lot in the Wadi Rum desert in Jordan **(illustration 10b)** and the post-production of the film and the re-shooting of certain shots took place in August 2018.

Here, too, the story is based on the elements of the original Middle Eastern folktale, and the plot shows many similarities with it, but of course it is also different. The two central characters are the titular Aladdin himself (Mena Massoud - *"The Royal Treatment"*) **(illustration 10c)**, the orphaned young poor street child who spends his dreary days with his little monkey Abu in the beautiful city of Agrabah and lives mostly by stealing. The other main character of the movie is the mysterious genie (Will Smith - *"Men in Black"* films etc...) **(illustration 10d)**, who after a long time gets out of the lantern again after the boy rubs it. The plot itself begins even before the two "paths" cross **(illustration 10e)**, when Aladdin meets the beautiful Princess Jasmine (Naomi Scott - *"Power Rangers"*) in the city market **(illustration 10f)**, who of course immediately charms him and as it soon turns out, the girl is not indifferent to the boy either. It would be quite difficult for me to tell you more without spoilers, so I would just say that there will be no shortage of complications, emotions, action, music and of course humor. After the story gets off to a good start, it continues to build and the film abounds in the rich plot and happenings, all the way to the end, and throughout provides a very entertaining and incredible visual experience **(illustration 10g)**.

Originally, Disney did not want a "traditional" remake, which, even if it follows the original story somewhat, tells it in a non-linear fashion. Presumably, this is why they saw fantasy in Guy Ritchie, because on the one hand he is not a "traditional" filmmaker (if I may put it that way), and on the other hand his films so far are not always completely linear, that is there are many jumps in time in his movies and also summaries at the end of the films. But we've gotten used to this, since it's one of his trademarks that we've come to expect from him after so much exceptional work, because once you get a feel for his style, you'll start watching his new films with this mindset. Of course, this direction could not avoid the comparison even now - just like in the case of *"Swept Away"*, *"Sherlock Holmes"* or even *"King Arthur"* - and many compared it to the 1992 animated film, which could be expected, but what can be said is that it remained largely faithful to the tale and the original story. Regardless, the fun is better, if we don't force the comparison too much and are open to innovations and accept the fact that even though it's still a remake, it's still a separate film, which does have a right to exist and it really worked out fantastically. In this, of course, also played a big role - in addition to the director - the cinematographer Alan Stewart *("Allies")* and his dazzling shots, as well as the editing work of James Herbert, who for the seventh time now provided his well-known expertise for Guy Ritchie film.

The film received mixed reviews from fans and critics alike. The actors received a lot of praise, the audience especially liked Smith, Massoud and Scott's excellent performance, - who showed improvised acting in more than one scene - as well as the period oriental-inspired costumes, the classy and rich sets and of course the beautiful soundtrack. At the same time, the film received negative reviews due to the rather large use of CGI and how Marwan Kenzari played Jaffar *("Black Adam")***(illustration 10h)**. According to the bad language, there was nothing memorable in it and even his parrot, Iago, was more entertaining than him **(illustration 10i)**. I would like to add here that I don't think there was a major problem with any of them, but maybe this is my biased opinion, everyone should decide for themselves. Billy Magnussen *("Tell me a story")*, who played Prince Anders, did not get away with it either when it came to criticism. Many fans considered his completely new character unnecessary, some even complained that he was played by a white actor **(illustration 10j)**. And speaking of the new characters, this is also true for Daliara, Jásmin's assistant, chief confidant and best friend, brought to life on screen by the also light-skinned Iranian-American actress Nasim Pedrad, who, like Scott, is also very beautiful *("Corporate Animals")* **(illustration 10k)**.

Disney has always insisted on keeping the elements of the original soundtrack, and thanks to the dedication of composer Alan Menken *("Beauty and the Beast", "Pocahontas", "The Little Mermaid")*, who has an extremely talented and extensive professional background - and has collaborated with the studio for a long time -, this is succeeded. Completed with several new recordings, a magnificent musical composition was created for the film, which perfectly match the excellent voices of Massoud and Scott, and which songs are simply beautiful and a pleasure to listen to them. The new composition called Speechless immediately stole into the hearts of the fans and immediately became people's favorite, but the *„Prince Ali"* song was also highlighted by many people from the soundtrack album. *„Arabian Nights"* is still a big favorite of mine since I was a child and it gives me a very pleasant feeling every time I hear it. Will Smith also excels in music scenes, but this is natural from a successful actor rapper. The dance sequences are also skillfully and spectacularly choreographed, the Prince Ali scene featured around 1,000 dancers and extras.

The novel version was released on 19 April 2019, exactly one month before the film was released in UK cinemas, courtesy of Disney Publishing Worldwide. The film debuted a day earlier on May 8 at Le Grand Rex in Paris, which is a popular cinema and concert venue. Aladdin had its first regional premiere in Jordan on May 13, 2019, and also Prince Ali bin Hussein and Princess Rym Ali paid their respects at the screening. As mentioned earlier, with this film, Ritchie not only made his 10th films, but also entered the club of billion-dollar filmmakers in terms of the production's revenue. The first live-action version of Aladdin in the 21st century has earned about 1 billion 50 million dollars worldwide so far with a budget of 180 million, which made it 8th on the list of the highest-grossing films of 2019 and Disney's 3rd most successful readaptation.

After all, Will Smith still knows how to act well, and Ritchie knows how to direct. Most people probably have fond memories of the original animated film, which was made more than 30 years ago, and this new creation can really bring up the old feelings. Aladdin, Genie, Jasmine, Abu, the flying Carpet, Iago, Jaffar or Rajah the tiger were defining characters in the childhood of many **(illustration 10l)**.

In any case, the majority of Aladdin fans are certainly very grateful to Ritchie and Disney for this film and will sit down to watched the second part with the same interest, which is planned to be released in cinemas in 2025 and is rumored that also will be directed by Mr. Ritchie. I'm really looking forward!

10a

10b

10c

10d

10e

10f

10g

10h

10i

10j

10k

10l

The Gentlemen (2019)

After the great success of Aladdin, in the same year, on December 3, 2019, Guy Ritchie's gangster film Gentlemen was shown for the first time at a VIP screening at the Curzon Mayfair cinema in London. It is perhaps one of the last really big films that cinemas all over the world could schedule before the Covid epidemic that broke out in the spring of 2020. It started in Great Britain on January 1 and in America on January 24, and from then on the world got to know Mickey (Matthew McConaughey - *"Interstellar"*), Ray (Charlie Hunnam), Fletcher (Hugh Grant) the coach (Colin Farrell - *"Daredevil"*) and their story. Since March of that year, the world has changed radically, and film production has changed with it, the writer's and filmmaker's union strikes follow one another, which halt and delay many productions, which, unfortunately, is often reflected in the quality. From this point of view, The Gentlemen was a fortunate work, which still belongs to the old era, many consider it the director's best film since *"Snatch"*, which was presented roughly 20 years earlier.

The 1 hour and 53 minute crime action film, which, like *"Lock"* and *"Snatch"*, contains several funny scenes - mainly thanks to the well-written dialogues between the well-created characters -, was produced by Ritchie, Bill Block and Ivan Atkinson. The latter in addition to Ritchie and Davis, also wrote the film. The movie was made under the auspices of STX Films, Ritchie Toff Guy Films and Miramax, and there is a smiling and imaginative reference to the latter at the end of the film, which was excellently incorporated into the story and a great advertisement for the production company.

Filming began in the fall of 2018, in November, and scenes for the film were recorded at locations such as the Longcross studio in Surrey, where Aladdin was partly filmed, and the Brompton Cemetery, where the director also made some shot for the first part of the Sherlock Holmes in 2008 **(illustration 11a)**. In addition to these, the staff worked in the studio of West London Films and in the multicultural part of London - in the western part of the city -, also in Sheperd's Bush, namely in The Princess Victoria pub, which was Mickey's gathering place in the film **(illustration 11b)**.

It is no coincidence that many people compare the production to Ritchie's first two films, since the story structure here is also partly framed by the narration of one person, in this case it is Fletcher (Hugh Grant) **(illustration 11c)**. He is the one try to sell his investigation material to Raymond (Charlie Hunnam) **(illustration 11d)** - or let's call it blackmail -, which could be also an excellent screenplay, meanwhile leads the film to the point where several important characters are involved in the chain of events, such as the coach (Colin Farrell) **(illustration 11e)**. According to the basic story, Mickey (Matthew McConaughey) **(illustration 11f)**, a successful cannabis trader of American origin who has been living in England for a long time, plans to retire early. He wants to sell his business - which he estimates is worth 400 million British pounds -, to a competing businessman Matthew (Jeremy Strong - *"The Big Short"*) **(illustration 11g)**.

After the offer is made, of course, thanks to greed and the desire for profit - or just because this is the nature of criminals - other applicants appear on the scene and the tough game and hustle begins among others with robbery, threats, blackmails and fights. There is everything here that cannot be missing from a real action-packed movie based on an underworld theme. A professional hip-hop dancer London rap band with checkered tracksuit from a boxing club (Toddlers) **(illustration 11h)**, rural English lords who rents out their property to marijuana plantation

(illustration 11i), a Russian mobster, heroin users, teenage street thugs and many other figures who complete and add color to the story that comes together like a puzzle at the end of the film.

The film has grossed over 115 million globally from a budget of just 22 million, making it 71st out of 200 on boxofficemojo.com's 2019 Wordwide list (where Aladdin was 9th) and ahead of films like for example, Stephen King novel adaption, *"Doctor Sleep"* (92nd place) or the Adam Sandler movie, *"Uncut Gems"* (117th place).[4] The actors in the film give excellent performances one by one and the casting was excellent, Ritchie managed to create one of the best actor crew of recent years. Matthew McConaughey was simply born to play Mickey. He plays the role of the elegant gangstar with incredible experience and his usual acting professionalism, who will do anything for his wife, dresses stylishly and elegantly, is generally respectful, but knows no mercy on occasion. Charlie Hunnam's cold intellect and mysterious gaze are almost frightening, he is the character you can guess from the very beginning that there is much more behind the sophisticated language and Mickey-like elegant

---

[4] https://www.boxofficemojo.com/year/world/2019/

appearance and he is also a character, who you don't want to pick up a quarrel with.

Colin Farrell also gives an exceptional performance in the role of the trainer in checkered tracksuits, who feels a special empathy for the street children and would do anything for his sons in the boxing gym, stealing almost every scene in which he appears. In addition to him, a big surprise is Hugh Grant, who takes care of almost all of the more humorous scenes, of course, primarily because of the dialogue that is nothing like. He plays the role of the sophisticated but extremely insidious blackmailer (Fletcher), who is crazy enough to blackmail London's one of the toughest underworld figures. It can be declared that Grant gives one of the best performances of his career in The Gentlemen **(illustration 11j)**. Eddie Marsan *("Sherlock Holmes")*, who plays Fletcher's "accomplice", also appears on the screen, brings his usual performance and is responsible for the funniest scene at the end of the film. The sound he makes... I have to laugh every time I think about it **(illustration 11k)**.

The female protagonist was also an excellent choice, well-known Michelle Dockery from *"Downton Abbey"* also excels as Mickey's wife, Rosalind is the perfect embodiment of the saying that behind every successful man is a strong woman **(illustration 11l)**. Henry Golding *("Crazy Rich Asians")* proved to be more than suitable for playing Dry Eye, he is one of the most negative characters **(illustration 11m)**. The other Asian actor, Tom Wu - who had previously worked with Ritchie in King Arthur -, also provides an authentic performance as the leader of the rival gang, he plays Lord George, Dry Eye's uncle **(illustration 11n)**.

In addition to its commercial success, The Gentlemen received mostly positive reviews, and not just one viewer feels the same way about the film and the director as this extremely satisfied fan, who said after the cinema: "He's the best in the business and if he only did these for the rest of his career I'd be a very happy man. This is an excellent movie well worth your time and money."[5] /jtindahouse, IMDB, January 1, 2020/ What might have been a negative criticism was related to individual twists in the film, according to which those who watch the whole movie can guess some of them in advance, but this might just be strain at a gnat. As is when someone complained about what happened to the Russian mobster after the raid happened, which is - at least I think -, completely irrelevant to the story and the central characters. Apart from these, it was really hard for even the critics to find

[5] https://www.imdb.com/title/tt8367814/reviews/?ref_=tt_ql_2

something, and some fans even called it better than the *"Lock"* or the *"Snatch"*.

The diverse film score was provided by composer Christopher Benstead - who received an Oscar for his work in *„Gravity"* in 2014 -, and songs by great artists such as the English badass Bugzy Malone (Ernie) - who also appeared in the film **(illustration 11o)** -, but we can also hear Vivaldi's Four Seasons, performed by violist Nigel Kennedy and the English Chambers Orchestra. Just as with *"Aladdin"*, Ritchie worked with editor Alan Stewart and cinematographer James Herbert, but the latter was joined by Paul Machliss *("Go,Baby,Go")*, who last showed his commitment to the profession in last year's DC movie, *"Flash"*.

It is interesting that the main female role and Mickey's wife was originally to be played by Kate Beckinsale *("Pearl Harbor")*, but later the choice fell on Michelle Dockery. The project was first presented at the 2018 Cannes Film Festival by CAA Media Finance (Creative Artists Agency), where Miramax immediately acquired the distribution rights. A spin-off television series is under development at Netflix, which will presumably present the prequels of the film and the first two parts of which will certainly be directed by Ritchie. The project is expected to be released this year (2024) starring Theo James *(Divergent)*, Vinnie Jones, Kaya Scodelario *("The Maze Runner")* and Giancarlo Esposito *("Breaking Bad")*. The Gentlemen is one of the few films that make you busy and curious, and while surrendering to its atmosphere, you already know that this is an another level. The perfect acting, the brilliantly written characters and dialogues, the story carefully constructed by the director and his co-writers, the plot threads slowly intertwining form a mixture that provides the audience with two hours of entertainment, which is really rare nowadays. It's basically fast-paced and exciting, but it slows down enough where it needs to be, but still doesn't get boring. It is characterized by deep, smart and meaningful dialogues, but it does not explain too much. The film does not take itself too seriously and thus does not turn into a parody of itself. It doesn't want to look like any movie that similar, even if it follows somewhat in the tradition of the *"Lock"* and the *"Snatch"*. It is a real British gangster film, but completely unique in its genre. It's elegant and sophisticated, but not fop or naff. In short, a true Guy Ritchie movie to the core.

11a

11b

11c

11d

11e

11f

11g

11h

11i

11j

11k

11l

11m

11n

11o

Wrath of Man (2021)

In 2021, the director continued, to the delight of many, what he had restarted with *"The Gentlemen"* two years before, after a gap of several years. He continued what most people probably know him about, continued to do what he did best since the beginning of his career, the production of crime-themed films. The triumvirate was reunited and Ritchie made his twelfth film, this time again with Ivan Atkinson and Bill Block, (and this is the second one for the three of them together) the Wrath of Man, also produced by Miramax, supplemented with MGM. Originally, the film was to be shown in America on January 15, but due to the Covid epidemic that has been going on for almost a year, the presentation was postponed to May 7, while in most countries it was already possible to see from April 22. The 1 hour 59 minute crime action thriller was released in UK cinemas from 23 July.

The film was made based on Nicolas Boukhrief's 2004 French film *"Cash Truck"* and its original story, which, in addition to the director, - as previously with Gentlemen - Ivan Atkinson and Marn Davies reworked and rethought it for a true Hollywood style, fast-paced and extremely action-packed modern revenge thriller. In addition to the writers and producers, Ritchie worked with almost the same crew as in his previous film, the flawless visual world was taken care of by cinematographer Alan Stewart and editor James Herbert this time too. And the music, which is mostly mysterious and fits the events perfectly, is again thanks to Christopher Benstead.

The main role is played by Jason Statham, he plays Patrick Hill, a harsh and mysterious driver, known only as H by his colleagues, who starts working for the Los Angeles cash-in-transit company called Fortico and it soon becomes clear that he is very good with weapons. I would reveal as many spoilers that it is not by chance that H starts working at the security company where one of the trucks recently became the victim of a fatal raid. The story, which Ritchie divided into four acts, begins to build quite dynamically during the ominous robbery and H's employment, which will be the start of a series of events. Just like the entire storytelling, the individual parts are not always linear either in the film and this makes it less predictable. We can see many flashbacks or the presentation of past events, all of which serve as an explanation for the present, but we have become accustomed to this from the director, and he still very cleverly and extremely thoroughly provides us the necessary information, which is essential for the enjoyment of the film as a whole.

Any further story or description of the plot would really be a spoiler, but I can tell you that his first film based on a one-man revenge campaign is not another security van movie filled with robberies. It is more like a work that partly presents psychological and serious moral dilemmas, during which the viewer also raises many important questions about it how he or she would act in certain situations. This plus makes this film unique within its genre, and this educational goal is what Ritchie always tries to sneak into the stories he tells in most cases, and among other things, this addition make him a unique director. Most of the film's scenes were shot in Los Angeles **(illustration 12a)**, and many shots recorded on the streets or in the armored cars **(illustration 12b)**.

In addition to Statham **(illustration 12c)**, who brings his character to perfection and who is perfectly suited to the role of H - with this film he worked with Ritchie for the fourth time, the last time in 2005's *"Revolver"* 16 years before -, several good actor still appears on the screen. First of all, I would immediately mention Holt McCallany *("Fight Club")*, who plays Bullet, the trainer of security workers and drivers, who also trains H for the job **(illustration 12d)**.

Then we have Scott Eastwood *("Suicide Squad")*, who is the main negative character in the film, his performance is also very good, he authentically shapes the veteran Jan **(illustration 12e)**. He is also a person who, with his companions, including the mercenary robbers Sam (Raúl Castillo - *"Army of the Dead"*) **(illustration 12f)** or Tom (Chris Reilly - *"The Feed"*) - who are also ex-soldiers -, **(illustration 12g)** would do anything for money.

Their leader is Jackson, who is portrayed by Jeffrey Donovan - who has been noticed by many since the *"Sicario"* films and the "Fargo" series -, best known to many from *"Low & Order"*. Among the robbers, he is perhaps the one whom the viewer can identify the best with, the actor plays very well the role of the sergeant who unites the mercenaries, who rather functions as a family man between the individual robberies **(illustration 12h)**.

After the films of *"Sherlock Holmes"* and *"The Gentlemen"*, the director has also cast Eddie Marsan in the movie, he is the immediate superior of the people working at the company. Unlike his previous characters, he is rather determined, who tries to think clearly and rationally even in difficult situations **(illustration 12i)**. Not so like

Boy Sweat Dave - brilliantly brought to life by Josh Hartnett *("Pearl Harbor")* -, who will be H's companion during the very first ride, and unlike whom he doesn't really know what to do with life-threatening situations **(illustration 12j)**. In some of the quieter scenes, Andy García *(„The Godfather III")* also appeares - who plays agent King -, makes the movie even more colorful with his usual honest intellect **(illustration 12k)**.

Among the female characters, I would highlight Niamh Algar *("Raised by Wolves")* who plays Dana, who is not only a pleasant sight among the many men, but her character is very likable. The actress perfectly portrays the tomboy girl trying to fit in a masculine profession, who, despite her occupation, can also function as a woman if necessary **(illustration 12l)**. Furthermore, we can see the beautiful Belgian actress, Lyne Renée (Kristy), already could familiar to Ritchie fans from *"The Gentlemen"*, she provides H with secret information, thereby helping him in his revenge campaign **(illustration 12m)**.

The Wrath of Man generally received mixed reviews from the critics, but it can be said that audiences and fans liked the director's new collaboration with Mr. Statham. The formers praised the fun action scenes and the rich visuals, while many of the latter missed the director's usual great dialogues. The film scored 67% based on 259 reviews on Rotten Tomatoes, a website that aggregates film reviews and opinions.[6] Matt Zoller Seitz of RogerEbert.com was enthusiastic, rating the film four out of four stars and calling it one of the director's best directed films and one of his least surprising in terms of style and tone. And he describes the presentation of Statham's character as similar to Clint Eastwood's Western films. This is what he wrote about the film:

„Gone is the jumpy, busy, lighthearted, buzzed-bloke-in-a-pub-telling-you-a-tale vibe of film like Snatch, RocknRolla, The Man from U.N.C.L.E., King Arthur: Legend of the Sword, and the like. In its place is voluptuous darkness, so sinister that you may wonder if its main character is the devil himself..."

The Total Film cinema newspaper had this to say about it in its special Christmas issue:

„The cast, which includes Josh Hartnett, Andy García, and for a brief but memorable moment, rapper Post Malone, chew the scenery with over-the-top, '80s- action-flick gusto, and the whole affair zips along with caffeinated vigour."[7]

---

[6] https://www.rottentomatoes.com/m/wrath_of_man
[7] Ken McIntyre: Wrath of Man. Total Film. London, 2021 Christmas, 102. pages

In terms of its theme, some say the film is very similar to the 2009 *"Armored"* movie, which was directed by the Hungarian Nimród Antal, while others compared it to the 2018 film *"Den of Thieves"* starring Gerard Butler and 50 Cent. This is only partially true, because anyone who has seen all three films can see the difference. In addition to the fact that each film is an excellent work, Ritchie's direction has a deeper content than the previous ones and, in addition to a lot of action and gunfire, it also contains a lot of moral teaching. The film had a budget of 40 million dollars and earned a total of nearly 104 million dollars, of which 3 million dollars on the first day of screening and 8.1 million dollars on the first weekend in America.

So the film is not another Statham action, it is much more than that. In the 4 acts, the movie perfectly balances the not always linear narrative. In addition to the plenty of action, it fits perfectly, the more emotional part presented in the numerous flashbacks or the justice provider scene, to which the perfect music gives the sometimes creepy atmosphere. It is typically a film in which the viewer grips the arm of the cinema chair throughout, thanks to the excellent tension.

Not to mention the well-written characters and brilliant acting, Statham delivered one of, if not the best work of his career, but the same can be said for the director. A must for anyone who loves them. Another proof that the pair of Guy Ritchie and Jason Statham is still a guarantee of success. Due to decades of friendship and perhaps his performance in Wrath of Man, there was no question that the director would also choose Jason for his next film, which is none other than "Operation Fortune", the ferocious action-comedy presented in 2023.

12a

12b

12c

12d

12e

12f

12g

12h

12i

12j

12k

12l

12m

Operation Fortune: Ruse de Guerre (2023)

The penultimate piece of Guy Ritchie's directorial/film repertoire to date is the 2023 spy action comedy Operation Fortune. This is the third film after *"The Gentlemen"* and *"Wrath of Man"*, which is the result of the director's joint collaboration with Miramax and STX Film, which began in 2018. AZ Celtic Films also joined the two film companies making the production, which, among others, is partly responsible for the „*Argo*" and *"Tinker, Taylor, Soldier, Spy"* starring Gary Oldman.

Like the previous two films, the director wrote the screenplay with Ivan Atkinson and Marn Davis, and the main producers of the 1 hour 54 minute film, - which give a lot of humour for the viewer -, are Ritchie, Atkinson, Bill Block, Steven Chasman *("Blitz ", "Bank job")* and the main character of the production, Jason Statham **(illustration 13a)**.

In addition to *"The Stath"*, the most important roles are played by great actors such as Hugh Grant (Greg Simmonds), who worked with the director for the third time **(illustration 13b)**, Cary Elwes (Nathan - *"Robin Hood: Men in Tights"*) **(illustration 13c)**, or the beautiful Aubrey Plaza (Sarah - *"Dirty Grandpa"*) **(illustration**

13d). After The Gentlemen, the director assigned another role to Bugzy Malone ("JJ") **(illustration 13e)** and also gave Josh Hartnett (Danny) another opportunity to show his talent again **(illustration 13f)**. Along with them, Eddie Marsan also appears on the screen (Knighton) **(illustration 13g)**, who with this role already colors Ritchie's film with his excellent performance for the fifth time.

The story is pretty much that there is a spy, Orson Fortune (Statham), who is tasked with get back a stolen super-technological device that, if it falls into the wrong hands, could lead to the change and upheaval of the world order. Sarah, the computer genius (Plaza), JJ the sniper (Malone), and Danny (Hartnett), a famous Hollywood actor in the film - as well as in real life - will help him in the mission. The latter is rather playing a bait role to impress, or more precisely, to involve the rich billionaire businessman Greg (Grant) in the web of events.

The premiere of the film took place on January 3, 2023 in Madrid, Spain, in Turkey on January 13, while in the USA it was shown on March 3, and in Great Britain it could be viewed from april 7 on Amazon Prime Video. The international release was originally planned much earlier, for January 21 and March 18, 2022, but the release of the film had to be postponed due to the ongoing Russian-Ukrainian war (today date is January 9, 2024). This was done because, according to the original story, Ukrainian antagonists would have appeared in the movie and because of the war that broke out in the meantime (February 24, 2022) - which caused general outrage worldwide - STX and the film's producers thought that the film needed to be restructured and then after that the currently existing version was completed.

So the cast is absolutely fine and it's suitable for all ages and gender, everyone can get the most likable character for him or her. There's a charming action hero (Statham), a popular movie star (Hartnett), a hot and clever IT girl (Plaza), a narcissistic power-obsessed gun dealer (Grant) and a cold-headed tough guy who is also a deadly sniper (Malone). All five give excellent acting performances and bring their characters authentically, but the viewers can't complain about the supporting characters either, everyone is in their place and plays relatively restrained, but with sufficient experience. Most of the scenery have a classy effect, the clothes are elegant and expensive, the cars and motorbikes are fast, and the landscapes are impressive.

The camera was filmed in such beautiful locations as, for example, the fabulous Cannes **(illustration 13h)**, Madrid

(illustration 13i), Antalya **(illustration 13j)**, Morocco **(illustration 13k)** or Doha **(illustration 13l)**.

The film received both positive and negative reviews, and neither the critics nor the viewers dealt gently with it. John Li, a staff member of Geek Culture, a website that reviews computer games, series and movies, rated the movie 7.4 out of 10 and thought the plot was good and the way Ritchie made the movie, especially highlighting Statham's character:

"Fortune is probably not the most realistic character we've seen on the big screen, but you can bet he is oozing with charisma."[8] He also said that we don't watch spy movies to believe that their superpowers exist in real life anyway.

Audiences polled by cinemascore.com gave the film an average grade of "B+" on a scale of A+ to F. Overall, people liked the film, praised the cast and Statham, but there were those who missed the director's distinctive style and didn't think that the first half of the film was very eventful. They're right, this Guy Ritchie direction is a bit different from the previous ones.

Unlike *"The Gentlemen"* and *"Wrath of Man",* for example, it doesn't have as much violence, and what it

---

[8] https://geekculture.co/geek-review-operation-fortune-ruse-de-guerre/

does have isn't showed to the viewer on the same level as in those movies. If I had to choose, Operation Fortune is closer to *"The Man from U.N.C.L.E"* than to the previous ones and not just because of the spy theme. Here, too, there is a lovable and somewhat funny team, antagonists aiming for world domination and a plot of restrained intensity, slower parts and suddenly fast-paced scenes follow each other.

The CGI effects are also very well done, there aren't too many of them, and the scenes shot at the original locations are also nicely shot, and the cuts are also fine. The amount of action is just enough, neither too much nor too little, and the choreography is also excellent. Anyone who likes to watch Statham fight can be happy, there will be no shortage of punch-ups.

Just as in Ritchie's previous film „*Wrath of Man*", we have composer Christopher Benstead to thank for the varied soundtrack album, which contains 15 extremely catchy tracks. Furthermore, cinematographer Alan Stewart and editor James Herbert have had the honor of lending their name and work again to another Guy Ritchie film. While Mr. Stewart for the fourth time, Mr. Herbert worked with the famous director for the 10th time in a row, and of course both delivered an excellent performance this time as well.

Home Cinema Choice newspaper wrote about the film:

„Guy Ritchie is nothing if not a visual stylist, and coupled with energetic cinematography from Alan Stewart (who also lensed Ritchie's The Gentlemen, Wrath of Man and Aladdin), the result is a Panavision treat. Various international locations are consistently colour-rich (no denuded palette here), and there's some neat specular highlights too. Sound: Even in this 5.1 guise (it was mixed theatrically in Dolby 7.1), the film's sound design, and score by Chris Benstead, is often inspired."[9]

The film was originally intended to be titled Five Eyes, but was later renamed Operation Fortune: Ruse de Guerre in September 2021. The film brought in only 37.85 million dollars against a budget of 50 million, so financially it has not been very successful so far, but of course the creators and Lionsgate - the distributor of the film - with subsequent DVD and blue-ray sales and various broadcasting rights, may they can still reach the amount spent at the beginning.

---

[9] SM: Show me the MacGuffin. Home Cinema Choice. Queenborough, 2023/5, 96. pages

It can be stated that Operation Fortune is made for the general public and can provide real entertainment to anyone who likes movies like „*James Bond*" or „*Mission Impossible*".

So anyone who wants to watch a really exciting action comedy with some spy feeling, an excellent cast, many beautiful and elegant locations, lots of substantial dialogue, fights, shootings, explosions, car chases and a lot of humour, will not be disappointed. Ritchie - who is currently very busy and is working on several projects at the same time - in the last of his completed films so far, is reaching for a new genre. After the presentation of exciting underworld stories, detective adventures, a fairy tale adaptation and spy films, he will now try his hand in a war drama, goes to Afghanistan to tell the exciting and touching story of two men in an extraordinary way.

13a

13b

13c

13d

13e

13f

13g

13h

13i

13j

13k

13l

Guy Ritchie's The Covenant (2023)

The last of the director's films released so far is the war action film The Covenant, released in the United States on April 21, 2023. The 2 hour and 3 minute movie - set mainly in Afghanistan -, is Guy Ritchie's most emotional direction to date since 2002's Swept Away and 2019's Aladdin. The film, which is about camaraderie, patriotism, and humanity, among other things, immediately became an audience favorite when it was released and is considered by many the best war-themed film of recent years. This title - in addition to the direction -, is presumably due to the amazing performances of the two main actors, Jake Gyllenhaal *("The Day After Tomorrow")* **(illustration 14a)** and Dar Salim *("Black Crab")* **(illustration 14b)**. Furthermore, the story based on real events, the excellent shots and the writers' team (Ritchie, Atkinson, Davies) who have come together for the fourth time in a row also played a big role in this. The film was also produced by STX Films, in addition to the production companies Toff Guy Films and Spanish Fresco Films Service. The film was also produced by Ritchie and Atkinson, and Josh Berger *("Fantastic Beasts: The Secrets* *of Dumbledore")* and John Friedberg *("Ferrari")* also participated in making of the film.

The touching story deals with the ordeals of the American Sergeant John Kinley (Gyllenhaal) and the Afghan interpreter Ahmed (Salim) in the dreary mountains of Afghanistan teeming with the Taliban **(illustration 14c)**. In addition, we can also see scenes recorded on internal locations for a few cuts, some of which take place in America **(illustration 14d)**. The production team announced in October 2021 that Jake Gyllenhaal will star in Ritchie's next film, whose American distribution rights were purchased by MGM in January 2022.

The film was originally titled The Interpreter, as its subject is partly about the Afghan translators who helped the soldiers arriving in Afghanistan in the fall of 2001 with their work, and their number was approximately 50,000. The Americans promised visas and settlement to the heroic men and women - and their families - who risked their lives in many cases due to the confrontation with the Taliban, and of course the common goal was to overthrow the fanatical regime and liberate the country from extremist forces. The title of the film was later changed to Guy Ritchie's The Covenant, this was announced by the director himself in December 2022 and this was allegedly necessary because a film called The Interpreter had already been made in 2005.

Filming began in February 2022 in Alicante, Spain, with additional works also took place in Sax, Alto Vinalopo and Zaragoza (air base) **(illustration 14e)**. The film is undoubtedly carrie on their back by the two protagonists Gyllenhaal and Salim **(illustration 14f)**, the exceptional performance of the two and the bond between them is what forms the backbone of the film. Besides them, talented actors also appear on the screen - and add color to the otherwise very eventful, exciting and moving film - such as Alexander Ludwig *("Vikings")* who plays Sergeant Declan O'Brady **(illustration 14g)**, Jonny Lee Miller who is Colonel Vokes *("Trainspotting")* **(illustration 14h)**, the star of Banshee and The Boys, Anthony Starr (Eddie Parker) **(illustration 14i)** or even Emily Beecham *("Daphne")*, who is Kinley's wife Caroline **(illustration 14j)**. Each of them adds their own personality and acting talent to the film, their performances are understated and authentic. It's safe to say that Ritchie and casting directors Daniel Hubbard *("Captain Phillips")* and Cynthia Huffman *("In Dubious Battle")* did a great job to find them for their roles.

This film is also a clear proof that you can't wrong with Jake Gyllenhaal, he is still a very top-rated actor, and even one of the best in Hollywood. The way he portrays the purposeful and extremely brave Sergeant Kinley, who would do anything for the unit he leads, for those in trouble and for his country, is really impressive. If necessary, he leads and directs a team, plans and considers calmly and collectedly. If necessary, he is a loving husband and father, but if necessary, he can also go crazy and show his usual fearfully insane look. If necessary, he fights the Taliban abroad, but if necessary, he fights the bureaucratic system at home in his own homeland. Anyway, it is really a performance worthy of an award **(illustration 14k)**. Watching the excellent performance of him and the other actors in the film, it is impossible not to think of the soldiers fighting every day away from their homes and loved ones, who provide freedom to the free world that most people take for granted, even though it is not at all. Of course, for Jake's great performance, the supporting role of Salim is indispensable. He also gives an amazing performance, his act can comes as a surprise and who I think also played a big role in Gyllenhaal being able to get the most out of himself. I believe that we will also hear about him in the future and I don't think a serious professional recognition is out of the question for him either, it's really amazing how he played the interpreter in the film, the humble and relatively quiet Ahmed, who is also willing to do anything for his family **(illustration 14l)**.

The Covenant received mostly positive reviews from critics, and viewers praised it. This is also evidenced by the fact that 92% of those surveyed by PostTrak gave it a positive score, and 77% said they would recommend it. There was one viewer who commented on IMDB: "This movie is a cinematic masterpiece that leaves a lasting impact on the viewer. With its powerful storytelling and exceptional performances, it's no surprise that many are hoping it will receive an Oscar nod."[10] – (Frank-liesenborgs May 11, 2023)

Although the Oscar nomination was missed, but this type of opinion is not far from reality at all and you really have the feeling after watching it that it was a great movie and you were glad you watched it. I was the same way, I really liked it and I'm glad that it came my way in connection with the book, but I probably would have watched it anyway sooner or later, but not only because of the director, but also because of Gyllenhaal and the story.

---

[10] https://www.imdb.com/title/tt4873118/reviews/?ref_=tt_ql_2

After the *„Wrath of Man"* and *„Operation Fortune"*, composer Christopher Benstead has created a wonderful piece of music here as well, all 17 songs perfectly enhance the given scene. In order for the film to boast the richest possible visuals, this time cinematographer Ed Wild was in charge *("London has fallen")*, perfectly complying with the director's instructions, and the editing was done at the same level by James Herbert again.

The great positive and originality of the film is that, roughly in the middle of the production, we have the feeling - mainly due to the development of the story and the twist in the plot - as if another production is starting, which begin to be exciting in a different way and is capable of appearing on the screen in a different way to attracts the attention of the viewers. At the end, you get the feeling that you have seen two movies for the price of one. One of the director's most elaborated works. The film was released in British cinemas on June 20 after its American release in April, and the Amazon Prime Video streaming service began broadcasting it on the Internet in Spain on June 2. The production costs were approximately 55 million dollars, the work generated a total of 6 million dollars in the first weekend in the USA and Canada, and

21.6 million dollars internationally so far (January 2024). Nowadays, thanks to mass production, most people sit down to watch a movie in the cinema or in front of the TV at home with strong reservations, this work is finally able to offer something new and dispels all doubts in the viewer right from the first minutes. A new but successful attempt by the director, in which - unlike his latest few films -, his previously known trademarks can be found more. Not only will captivate you until the two hours playtime, but we will be thinking about the movie and on the story based on real events also later on, not to mention the information provided at the end of the film.

Guy Ritchie's Covenant is a great and unique film that tells an interesting and at the same time quite touching story about important subjects, such as justice, heroism, humanity and camaraderie, without going too preachy. It does this with understated but highly professional direction and an impeccably written script, with excellent acting, dazzling visuals and music, full of tension, action and adrenaline, and a lots of emotion. It is highly recommended for those who like war films, with serious moral content, important things to say and deep human stories. And for Ritchie fans, it's a must-see, it's simply not to be missed.

14a

14b

14c

14d

14e

14f

14g

14h

14i

14j

14k

14l

References

[1] pl: Lock, Stock and Two Smoking Barrels, Cinema magazine. Budapest, 1999/5, 67. pages.

[2] David Bordwell, Kristin Thompson, Jeff Smith: Film Art – An introduction. Twelfth edition. McGraw-Hill Education, 2020. 199. pages

[3] https://www.ign.com/articles/2008/09/02/rocknrolla-uk-review

[4] https://www.boxofficemojo.com/year/world/2019/

[5] https://www.imdb.com/title/tt8367814/reviews/?ref_=tt_ql_2

[6] https://www.rottentomatoes.com/m/wrath_of_man

[7] Ken McIntyre: Wrath of Man. Total Film. London, 2021 Christmas, 102. pages

[8] https://geekculture.co/geek-review-operation-fortune-ruse-de-guerre/

[9] SM: Show me the MacGuffin. Home Cinema Choice. Queenborough, 2023/5, 96. pages

[10] https://www.imdb.com/title/tt4873118/reviews/?ref_=tt_ql_2

Printed in Great Britain
by Amazon